WELCOME THE CHILD

A CHILD ADVOCACY GUIDE FOR CHURCHES

By Kathleen A. Guy

Cover photo by Nita Winter

ISBN: 0-938008-84-6
Library of Congress Catalog Card Number 90-085745

Contents

Acknowledgments

This book could not have been produced without the assistance and contributions of the following people:

• Shannon Daley, Carol Wehrheim, and Belva Finlay, who helped write and edit pieces of this book.

• Stephen Wilhite, who worked tirelessly to edit and retype hundreds of pages of text.

• Marian Wright Edelman, Margaret Schwarzer, Minerva Carcano, Ruth Fowler, Eileen Lindner, and Mary Potter Engel, who contributed sermons and other texts.

• Donna Jablonski, Janis Johnston, and David Heffernan, who produced this book.

• MaryLee Allen, Lisa Mihaly, Sara Rosenbaum, Helen Blank, Kati Haycock, Ray O'Brien, and Luis Duany, who provided research and input on Section III.

• The members of the Child Advocacy Working Group of the National Council of Churches, whose commitment to children and dedicated work on their behalf helped make this book possible.

PREFACE

Fear not this goodness as a thing impossible,
nor the pursuit of it as something alien, set
a great way off; it hangs on our own choice.

Fourth Century Desert Father

Three thousand three hundred and two years ago, the
Jewish Book of Commentaries said that before God
would give the people of Israel the Torah, God
demanded adequate guarantors. In response the people
offered their elders. But God said the elders were not
sufficient. When they offered their prophets, God also
rejected them as insufficient guarantors. Only when they
offered their children and promised to teach them God's
commandments did God agree to share the commandments.

Without children, there would have been no Covenant.
Without healthy, educated children, there will be no strong
American future or competitive work force.

The 1990s will be an era of struggle for America's con-
science and future. And people of faith have to be moral
guerrillas in that struggle. The battles will not be as dramatic
as Gettysburg or Vietnam, but they will shape our place in
the twenty-first century world no less. The bombs poised to
blow up the American dream, ideals, and social fabric ema-
nate from no enemies without. They are ticking away within
ourselves, our children, our families, in our loss of community, and in our national moral drift.

Nowhere is the paralysis of public and private con-
science more evident than in the neglect and abandonment
of millions of our children at a time when our nation faces a
shrinking pool of children and virtually all of the growth in
our child population will be poor and minority children. Between 1985 and 2000 white males will account for only 15
percent of the net additions to the labor force.

Despite a host of specific gains, much knowledge about
and examples of what works to prevent child deficits and
suffering, America's children and families of all races and
incomes are in increasing peril:

- Every eight seconds of the school day an American
  child drops out (552,000 during the 1987-1988 school
  year).
- Every 26 seconds of each day an American child runs
  away from home (1.2 million a year).
- Every 47 seconds an American child is abused or neglected (675,000 a year).
- Every 67 seconds an American teenager has a baby
  (467,623 in 1987).
- Every seven minutes an American child is arrested
  for a drug offense (70,000 a year).
- Every 30 minutes an American child is arrested for
  drunken driving (17,674 a year).
- Every 36 minutes an American child is killed or in-
  jured by guns (14,600 a year).
- Every 53 minutes an American child dies because of
  poverty (10,000 a year).

Is it acceptable to you as a person of faith that children
are the poorest Americans in the wealthiest nation on earth?
The United States has the highest child poverty rate among
eight industrialized nations in a recent study.

Do you think the leading world military power lacks the
capacity to rank first rather than nineteenth in keeping its
infants alive and cannot do better than forty-ninth in immu-
nizing its non-white infants against polio — behind
Botswana and Albania?

Does it offend your sense of national pride that our nation is not one of 70 nations that provide medical care to all
pregnant women, not one of the 63 nations that provide a
family allowance to mothers and their children, and not one
of 17 industrialized nations that provide parental leave
when a child is born, adopted, or sick?

Are we and our political leaders preparing a competitive
work force for the future when our children know less geography than children in Iran, less mathematics than children
in Japan, and less science than children in Spain?

We at the Children's Defense Fund seek, with your help, to create a new American paradigm in the 1990s which makes it un-American for any child to grow up poor, unsafe, without basic health care, nutrition, housing, a strong early childhood foundation, or the education they need to earn their share of the American dream.

We feel confident that we know *what* to do to alleviate child poverty and suffering. The challenge now is *how* to create the sense of urgency and the national and political will to give children first rather than last call on national, community, and family interests and resources. At the Children's Defense Fund we believe that committed individuals, organizations, and congregations can make life better for millions of children. The problems that too many of our nation's children see each day are very real — but they can be alleviated. Each and every one of us can help make a difference in the lives of children. And that's why your moral witness and hard work are so important.

Please use this *Guide to Child Advocacy* to involve yourself and others in making that difference in your home, church, community, city, state, and nation. Use **Section I: Looking at Children Through the Eyes of Faith** as you pray about and study the needs of children in your community, state, and around the nation. Our hope for children, ultimately, rests with God. It is God who gives us the faith and courage and strength to nurture and protect children. It is God who forgives us when we don't. Ask God for the compassion to see the faces and hear the cries of children behind the statistics and stories.

This Guide will help you involve your congregation in study and in action. Ministering through outreach in your community is vital. Look to **Section IV: Giving Voice to the Voiceless**, however, to learn how you can extend your advocacy beyond the community to make your voice, and the voices of children, heard in the public policy and political process. Ask God for the wisdom to know what we faithfully and realistically can do. Then get righteously angry. Get inspired. Get involved. Demand action.

In the Book of Micah we read: "And what does the Lord require of [us], but to do justice, and to love kindness, and to walk humbly with [our] God?" I ask you to join with me and millions of people of faith on this journey of celebrating and loving our own, our congregation's, and all of God's children, of taking on their joys and sorrows, of finding ways to help them grow and develop to their God-given potential, and of seeking justice for *all* of our nation's children. May God bless us on our journey. May we find joy and strength in one another as we join arm-in-arm with children.

Marian Wright Edelman

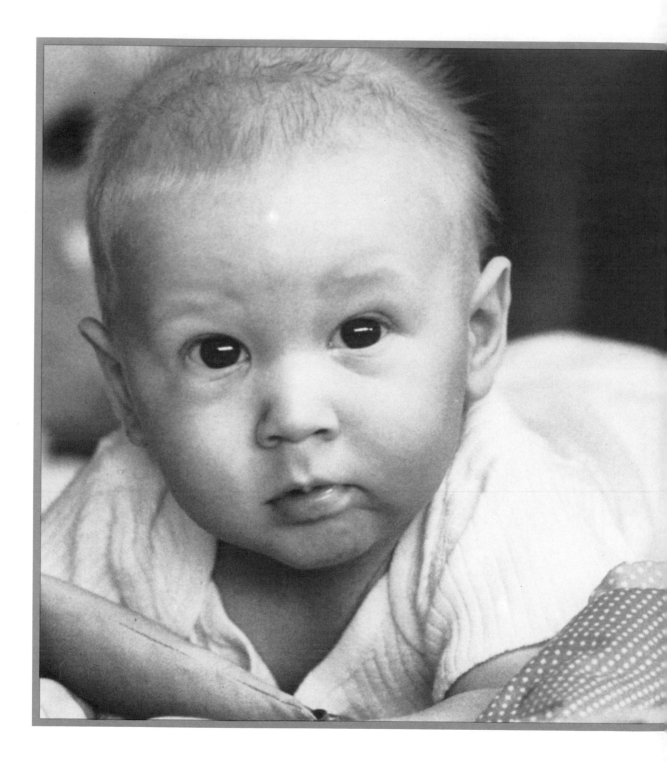

PHOTO BY KATHY SLOANE

STANDING STRONG FOR CHILDREN

How To Use This Guide

All people of faith acknowledge and practice, in various ways, the responsibility to nurture children. This book is intended in part to further that work: to help churches strengthen the role of children in the congregation; to affirm their growth, discoveries, and experiences; and to support their participation in the life of the congregation.

This book also aims to foster reflection on the many needs of children in the congregation, community, and around the nation, especially those who suffer in mind, body, and spirit. This book will help congregations develop or strengthen plans for children's ministries and child advocacy, and in so doing will deepen the congregation's understanding of our call and responsibility, as people of faith, to nurture, protect, and to advocate on behalf of the children.

All the biblical quotations found in this book are taken from the *New Revised Standard Version*.

Who Will Benefit From This Guide?

This guide is for:
- Clergy and staff;
- Church council and committee members;
- Members who work with and for children in a variety of roles — through the church, community, or professional involvement;
- Those church members not yet active on children's concerns; and
- Community child advocates who want to establish relationships with congregations and religious organizations.

It is hoped that this book will encourage networking among your congregation and other congregations, national religious organizations, community social service agencies and programs, and national child advocacy groups.

The Sections of this Book

The sections of this book have been written so that they build upon and strengthen each other. Together, they provide a more comprehensive approach to ministering to the varied needs of children in the church and in society. However, each section has been written so that it may be used on its own or in conjunction with another section or other resources. Your congregation may decide to use only a few of the sections or to divide them among clergy, staff, committees, groups, and members.

As you and your congregation use this book, please reflect on and evaluate which sections and resources are most helpful, and which might have been designed or developed in a more useful manner. An evaluation form has been provided at the back of the book. Your responses are invited sincerely so that we might in the future develop materials and resources to better help congregations minister to children.

By checking the box found at the bottom of the form and returning it to CDF, you and your congregation can elect to become part of a growing network of child advocates in congregations and in communities around the nation, enabling you to keep informed and share resources and ideas with one another.

STANDING STRONG FOR CHILDREN:

Teen Pregnancy

- Each year one in 10 teenage girls in the United States becomes pregnant, compared with fewer than one in 20 in England, France, or Canada, and one in 30 in Sweden.
- In 1970 three of 10 teenagers giving birth were unmarried. In 1988 two of three were unmarried.
- Two of five young women who drop out cite pregnancy or marriage as their reason for leaving school.
- About 1 million teenage girls get pregnant each year, and almost half a million babies (equivalent to the population of Boston) are born to teenagers.
- Only half the teenage girls who become parents before they reach 18 will be graduated from high school by their mid-twenties.

Education

- Every eight seconds of the school day an American child drops out (552,000 during the 1987-1988 school year).
- Among 16-year-olds who have lived at least half their lives in poverty, four of 10 have repeated at least one grade.
- Poor teenagers are four times more likely than nonpoor teens to have below-average basic academic skills.
- The Soviet Union, Hungary, Canada, and Norway spend more of their Gross National Product on education than does the United States.
- The reading and math skills of 17-year-old black and Latino students are comparable to those of white 13-year-olds.

Preschool

- Every $1 invested in high-quality preschool programs such as Head Start saves $6 in lowered costs for special education, grade retention, public assistance, and crime later on.
- The children enrolled in Head Start are more likely than other poor children to be literate, employed, and enrolled in postsecondary education.
- Head Start now serves approximately one in four eligible youngsters.

STORIES BEHIND THE STATISTICS:

Dahlia's Story:

Dahlia, a child of a teenage mother in one of the nation's poorest cities, could not escape the cycle of poverty. When she became pregnant at 16, she left her job at a bank and was supported by Julio, the father of her child. After her daughter Jennifer was born, Julio and Dahlia separated and Dahlia went on welfare.

Wayne's Story:

Wayne was tutored at Simpson United Methodist Church while he was in the seventh and eighth grades. He recalls, "When I first started tutoring I used to goof off and I didn't think it would help. I sat down with my tutor and he showed me how easy it was to learn. That's when I got interested and really started learning. Without tutoring, I would have failed some classes and not graduated from high school. I would have failed seventh and eighth grades."

Anne's Story:

Anne is a high school dropout who first became a mother when she was 16. She had six children by the time she was 26. She worked as a maid, and her husband worked as a store clerk.

IT MAKES A DIFFERENCE

ADVOCACY COMES IN MANY FORMS:

One Person

Through the help of a program called the Young Mothers Group, organized and run by a United Church of Christ minister, Dahlia received support and encouragement from her peers and the adult resource volunteers. "The Young Mothers Group helped me decide what I'm going to do with my life," said Dahlia. "Speakers come to talk to us about their careers and how they did it — and that encouraged me a lot. The group members are the same age as I am and they're also young mothers. It's encouraging to me because I feel I'm not the only one out there who's a teen parent."

ACHIEVEMENT IS NOT A STATISTIC

Through the weekly support of the Young Mothers Group, Dahlia and the other young mothers learned parenting skills, personal hygiene, and employment skills. Dahlia started working part time, 20 hours a week, and went back to school. While completing her education and supporting her young child, she knows that personal support and help is available weekly when she gathers with other young mothers — all because one person saw a need and found a way to help meet it.

A Group of Church Women

The United Methodist Women's Local Unit of Simpson United Methodist Church in West Virginia recognized the need to assist with the education of children 10 years ago. The group started a tutorial program in its church building that has expanded to 22 sites. Today the program is coordinated by the Charleston District Outreach Ministries of the United Methodist Church.

Each volunteer tutor receives training and support. After the students are tested and evaluated, tutors receive a "prescription" describing where to begin and what skills need reinforcing.

"Right now, I really thank my tutor because he really helped me out," says Wayne. "He pushed me towards the things that I wanted to do and the goals that I set. It's great to have someone like that who cares and helps kids."

Wayne recently graduated from high school and is making plans to build and market low-income housing on the land his grandmother left him in her will. Wayne's is one of many lives reversed because a group saw where help was needed and did something about it.

Churches Working to Change Public Policies

For 25 years the Head Start program, funded by the federal government, has been involving parents, teachers, and volunteers in a comprehensive child development program for disadvantaged three-, four-, and five-year-olds. Head Start also ensures that these children receive the health and supportive services they need to get off to an even start with other children in school and later life.

The religious community has been a strong advocate for full funding of the Head Start program so that all eligible children can participate. Many churches house Head Start programs. Local congregations write letters to their members of Congress requesting continued and increased funding for Head Start.

At 26 Anne went back to school and received her high school diploma. She enrolled her children in the Head Start program and was employed by Head Start as a part-time worker.

With encouragement and guidance from the Head Start staff, Anne went on to college and eventually completed her college degree. Anne's three oldest children have completed college and are employed. Her other three children now are attending college.

WHAT IS CHILD ADVOCACY?

Child advocacy is standing up for children—your own, and others'. It is an attitude, a process you go through, and all the steps along the way that bring about changes to help children grow and develop fully.

- If your child is suspended from school for being late three times and you go to the principal to discuss the problem together to get her back into school, you are engaging in child advocacy.
- If you go to the worship committee of your congregation to ask that children be included as greeters or ushers on Sunday mornings, you are being a child advocate.
- If you go to a PTA meeting to urge teachers not to track children, that too is advocacy.
- If you and others meet with the ruling body of your congregation to present a plan to use the church building and resources for a latch-key program, you are advocating for children.
- If you sign a petition to get a playground with safe equipment built in your neighborhood and a traffic light on the playground corner, that also is child advocacy.
- If you send a letter supporting your governor's promise to sign a law creating jobs for teenagers, or if you write to your senators and representative asking them to vote for a bill that makes more money available for day care or health care for children, you are participating in child advocacy.

PHOTO BY ERIC FUTRAN

LOOKING AT CHILDREN THROUGH THE EYES OF FAITH

HOW TO USE THIS SECTION

T he first step in becoming an advocate for children is to be aware of the place of children in the world and in the church today. Along with this awareness comes the recognition of God's love and care for all children, but especially for those who are most vulnerable and in need of care. For Christians, an important part of advocacy for children who are vulnerable and powerless is to seek God's will and guidance in prayer and meditation. So often what we do affects children, but we don't recognize either the positive or negative impact we are having at the time. God's grace can open our eyes and give us the strength and courage to do what is in our power to do for children.

This section provides meditations that can be used with committees, boards, councils, classes, or any group within the congregation to lift up the needs of children and our responsibility to them. Look through the meditations. Use those that are appropriate to your setting. Adapt them or develop your own. Reflection upon God's word and our call to discipleship on behalf of children is a necessary component of child advocacy for Christians, because every decision we make as individuals and as groups affects children in some way. These meditations and the accompanying questions for discussion will help you and the groups with which you meet consider what some of these effects may be.

In this section you also will find resources and suggestions for a Children's Sabbath Day. One way to bring the needs of children to the entire congregation is to plan a service of worship on the theme of children. A Children's Sabbath also can be adapted to an existing event to include the theme of child advocacy. See pages 29-38 for ways to incorporate the entire faith community into this celebration, including opportunities for raising awareness, involving the congregation in action, and reflecting on the mission of God.

Return to this section regularly as you stand strong for children in your congregation and community. Child advocacy is not a fad, but a lifetime commitment. To sustain your spirit and will, meditate and reflect regularly on what you are called to do on behalf of children.

For pastors and worship leaders and planners

In this section there are suggestions for hymns, prayers, scriptures, and other aspects of the liturgy. Throughout this book there are stories and informational material you may want to include in a sermon or print in the worship bulletin. A wealth of illustrations detailing ministries for children and God's call to us to care for the vulnerable and powerless in our midst can be found in the other sections.

For pastors and other members of the church staff

Your interest and involvement in child advocacy will do much to encourage your congregation to participate in this ministry. Recognizing and pointing out the needs of children as you meet with committees or in prayers or sermons throughout the year not only lends support to those who work for and with children, but validates their ministry as well. If you have time to do nothing more for children, consider them each time you prepare a sermon, lead a discussion group, or work with a committee. You are an important voice for children in the life of your congregation and your community.

CHAPTER 1

SERMONS, BIBLE STUDIES, REFLECTIONS

For meditation and discussion with:

- Committees and boards;
- Ruling bodies;
- Fellowship groups of young people or adults; and
- Church staff.

The readings in this section can be used in a variety of ways. Without the discussion questions they can be presented as meditations to begin a meeting. With the discussion questions they can raise a group's awareness of children's needs. By focusing the questions more specifically on your setting, you can help the group think about what is needed for the children of your congregation, your community, our nation, or the world.

IN YOUR HEART

Focus: We teach God's word to our children as we talk with them about our faith and as we minister in God's name in the world.

Scripture: Deuteronomy 6:4-9
Matthew 22:36-40

God's promise to our earliest ancestors in the faith was that God would be their God and that they would be God's people. Through the incarnation, death, and resurrection of Christ that promise became more intimate and the people of God began to call themselves children of God, joint heirs, adopted brothers and sisters with Christ.

Scripture is full of references to God as loving parent, and many of us find great solace and strength in the vision of ourselves as God's children. These images are powerful when the parent–child relationship we have experienced is one in which as children we received love, forgiveness, protection, food, shelter, clothing — all that is needed for spiritual and physical well-being. That is what we ask of God. And that is what children need from us.

If we have not experienced a positive, nurturing, and secure relationship between parent and child, we may instead have developed a powerful vision of what that bond ought to be in its most perfect form — the image of God as loving parent.

Reflecting on our own experiences as children — whether they were positive or negative — gives us insight into the awesomely important role of human parents. It deepens our compassion for children today who are not blessed with an experience of love, acceptance, security, and nurturing. And it underscores our charge to embody the qualities that God as our loving parent has revealed to us.

Each day many of our nation's children go without proper care. In our society, children are the poorest citizens. Every year 10,000 children die of effects of poverty. A baby born in this nation is less likely to reach his or her first birthday than a baby born in a much poorer country such as Singapore.

Many poor children who do survive grow up under a cloud of hopelessness. For more than 12 million children in the United States — one of five — childhood is a time when they and their families can think of little but basic survival.

Pervasive poverty threatens not only poor children, but also the social and spiritual fabric of our nation. The cost is dear. The very lives — the minds, spirits, and emotions — of these children are damaged and endangered. If we shut our eyes and refuse to see them we live in disobedience to God, whose word we have been commanded to teach to children — all children. Thus, our relationship with God suffers, for how do we teach a child of God's love when he or she does not know that love through us?

God's love can be known through us in personal relationships, and it also can be known in how we use the resources God has given us. Our task as Christians, whether adult, young person, or child, is to shape the world in which we live so that all people, whatever age, have what is required for spiritual and physical well-being. As we do this, we recite the word of God to children everywhere.

Love of God cannot be separated from love of neighbor. Few of our neighbors are as vulnerable as children. Children cannot fend for themselves. Children need our help, and they need our love. Children are powerless in the political decisions that shape their lives and futures. We are the ones with the ability and the opportunity to fulfill God's promise to them. As we work to improve their lives today and tomorrow, we are loving God with all our hearts, souls, and might.

Questions for Reflection and Discussion
- In what ways do you, your committee, or your congregation "recite [the word of God] to your children"?
- How do these actions — actions the children see or experience — show God's word?

- What more can you be or say? How can you show your love of God with all your heart, soul, and might by acting on behalf of children?

Prayer
We join with people of God through all the ages, declaring "The Lord is our God, the Lord alone." We seek your help, O God, as we struggle to keep your word to us in this time and place. Guide us as we seek to keep our actions consistent with your word to us. Keep us ever from failing to hold your word in our hearts and conveying it to the children of your world at every opportunity. Through Jesus Christ, the embodiment of your Word, we pray. Amen.

Based on a sermon by Kathleen A. Guy
Religious Affairs Coordinator
Children's Defense Fund
Washington, DC

THERE IS A BOY HERE

Focus: The adult community of faith can discover the Spirit of God through the gifts of children.

Scripture: John 6:1-14

The story of the feeding of the 5,000 is the story of God's realm made visible on this earth. Through God's mercy, the huge crowd was fed in fellowship and peace. The story is familiar, perhaps too familiar. We know it so well that we forget to listen as it is told or read. We know there were only five loaves and two fish and there were thousands to feed. But do we remember who provided the meager offering that fed the crowd? Oh yes, a boy, according to the Gospel of John.

Jesus didn't pull the loaves and fish out of the air. It was no slight-of-hand trick. He created a community feast by using what the community had to offer, what the boy had to offer. Jesus had the holy imagination to see the child's willingness to give and the potential abundance in his offerings.

One of the disciples, though observant enough to spot the child with his lunch, was too weary to imagine the divine potential presented. Andrew said, "There is a boy here who has five barley loaves and two fish. But what are they among so many people?"

What are they? In the story they are all that is needed. They are the ingredients touched by Jesus that would yield a bounteous feast for all gathered. Through Christ, who saw the transforming potential of the child's simple offering, the hungry and tired crowd discovered enough bread and fish to feed everyone.

Ironically, wonderfully, the belongings of one of the youngest, least powerful members of that mighty gathering turned out to be the instrument that inspired Christ's miracle that day. The wisdom of the world teaches us to focus on political power and might, but Christ points us to a child, once again.

Just as the boy and his bundle were the instruments of Jesus' miracle, we are invited to look for the potential miracles found in the hearts and souls of children, even the most unlikely children. They have gifts and talents that are waiting to be uncovered and nurtured.

The Holy Spirit has given each of us spiritual gifts of all varieties. Now it is our turn to recognize the gifts of the children in our world. It is our turn to reach out and uncover the gifts our children are offering. When we realize the potential of that which children have to offer, our faith community and our nation can be transformed by the miracle of their gifts.

Questions for Reflection and Discussion
- When has a child been a source of the knowledge of God in your life?
- Think about the children you know. What gifts of the Spirit do you discern in them?
- What, in your congregation, helps children use their gifts for the good of the community? What hinders them?

Prayer

God of all beings, large and small, old and young, we praise you for the gift of your Son, Jesus Christ, his life and his teachings. We thank you for the children in our congregation and in our lives. Help us to acknowledge their presence and their gifts, alert us to their potential as Jesus was alert to the potential of the boy with his meager lunch of loaves and fish. Remind us in our work together that we are blessed by you a hundredfold, as were those who came to hear your Son. Keep us mindful of all your people, young and old. Amen.

Based on a biblical reflection by Margaret Schwarzer
Intern from Yale Divinity School
Children's Defense Fund
Washington, DC

AT THE PACE OF CHILDREN

Focus: When we take notice of the pace of the children in our world, we recognize our need to adjust to their pace to be on the path to the kingdom of God.

Scripture: Genesis 33:12-14
Matthew 18:2-5

At first glance, this biblical narrative from Genesis gives us a positive image of Jacob carefully weighing the needs of children.

Yet, throughout the narrative of the reconciliation of Esau and Jacob, we have a vignette of people of faith using children. The children are treated as a buffer between Esau and Jacob, as chattel to be offered up as gifts in times of need, and as sacrifices in times of battle. Knowing something about the social attitude, traditions, and mores of the time gives us the broader picture of this treatment.

An ancient Pentateuchal tradition was that God would provide land and posterity for Israel. Jacob comes to be identified as the representative of the divine promise. To him are born the 12 sons of Israel, and his descendants gain hold of land in Shechem, in the area of Canaan. Land and posterity were of the highest importance, for they would determine Israel's ability to survive as a people. Children were viewed as a means to survival, not necessarily as persons of inherent worth. The meaning of the names of two of the women who bore children to Jacob illustrates the attitude toward women and children. In the ancient language the name Leah means "cow," and the name Rachel means "ewe"!

What's more, male children were considered more important than female children. For this reason we are more likely to remember that Jacob had 12 sons than we are to remember that he had 13 children, and that his twelfth child was not Benjamin, but a girl child named Dinah.

Other cultures of the time had similar attitudes toward children. For example, we know the Greeks did not want large families for fear that too many children would mean not enough food to feed everyone. So the Greek customs and laws condoned infanticide, and children often were left to die from exposure in the wilderness. In the time of Moses children often were abandoned in the Nile or Euphrates rivers.

The negative attitudes toward children had not changed significantly by the beginning of the Christian era. *The Interpreter's Bible* commentary on the Gospel of Matthew reports a letter written by an Egyptian laborer named Hilarion to his pregnant wife, Alis. Hilarion advises her, if she has a girl, to let the baby die.

Similarities in Jacob's and Christ's Perspectives on Children

There are two statements that Jacob makes when returning home, however, that point to a biblical understanding of children and our relationship with them that is positive, rather than negative.

The first of these statements comes when Esau sees the company of his brother Jacob and asks, "Who are these with you?" Jacob responds, "The children whom God has graciously given your servant" (Genesis 33:5). In so answering Jacob acknowledges the sacred worth of the children, because they are from God.

The second positive statement comes when Jacob says, "...I will lead on slowly, according to the pace of the cattle that are before me and according to the pace of the children..." (Genesis 33:14). Jacob's concern for walking at the pace of the children comes from their fragility and need for protection. His comment also suggests that children need to be heard and heeded by adults. On this point Jesus also teaches us.

In the Gospel of Matthew 18:1, the disciples come and ask Jesus, "Who is the greatest in the kingdom of heaven?" Jesus responds neither with a traditional theological answer, nor with a guidebook, nor with a formula for success. Jesus instead presents them with a child: "He called a child, whom he put among them, and said, 'Truly I tell you, unless you change and become like children, you will never enter the kingdom of heaven. Whoever becomes humble like this child is the greatest in the kingdom of heaven'" (Matthew 18:2-4).

A paradox is reflected in the two passages of scripture we have been considering. Jacob speaks of leading the children to the homeland as a father who knows what is best for them.

Jesus teaches that it is the children who will lead us to the homeland of God's eternal presence, and that in the children the measure of greatness is to be found.

This paradox continues in our lifetime. Yes, we must care for the children with whom God has blessed us — truly *care* for them. At the same time, we must be attentive to what the children have to say to us. Children lead us daily — if only we will listen.

Knowing What To Preserve

Children do not always set the best example; they can be self-centered and selfish. The apostle Paul stresses that as we mature there are certain child-like ways we must put behind us. But there are also qualities of children, qualities of humble nature, which Jesus recommends we consider and incorporate into our lives.

Some of those qualities are relationships of equality that are to be seen among children regardless of race, color, or social status; lack of worldly ambition; and a receptiveness to new things. Adults teach children to feel prejudice and racism, to lust for power and control, and to close their minds to the possibility of new things. Adults have set the pace for life as we know it today. Often that pace has been determined by overwhelming ambition. It is adults who must bear the moral and ethical responsibility for the condition of the world.

We would do well, as we approach the end of this century, to look to the children, and to learn from them. Our greatness will be determined by our ability to walk at their pace. It is, in fact, the children who will lead us to the kingdom of heaven.

Questions for Reflection and Discussion

- Think first about the way Jacob answered Esau. How was it a reversal of the norms of that time? How was Jesus' answer to his followers also a reversal of the norms of his time?
- As a nation, we talk about the importance of our children. Yet there are many children who are not included in that definition of importance. What would it mean to reverse the norm by which our nation lives, rather than speaks?
- What would it mean for your congregation, board, or committee to conduct its business "at the pace of children"? What changes in thinking would it necessitate?

Prayer

O Thou who blesses each of us, young and old, according to your loving kindness, grant us the capacity to find the pace of our children and to match it, so that we too may be headed toward your rule of peace and justice. Forgive us our desires to be first, best, and strongest, when we know that all life is in your hands. Remind us that we, too, are children in your sight. In the name of your Son, who showed us all good things. Amen.

Excerpts from a sermon by Minerva G. Carcano
District Superintendent of the
Western District
Rio Grande Conference United Methodist Church
Albuquerque, NM

Do Not Lose Heart

Focus: Changing an unjust law or situation requires faith and persistence.

Scripture: Luke 18:1-8

An adult, whether a parent or not, who has tried to withstand the pleadings of a child can identify with the judge in the parable. And any child who has found success by wearing down a parent, grandparent, aunt, or uncle knows the determination of the widow.

Although different from most of Jesus' parables, this one is consistent with Jewish teachings in Jesus' day, and may be illustrative of Proverbs 25:15: "With patience a ruler may be persuaded, and a soft tongue can break bones."

The widow and the proverb are important to us as we seek to provide justice for the children of our congregation, our community, our nation, and our world. But children, too, are examples to us by their persistence. When we feel downhearted for lack of progress, when we feel defeated after a hard-fought debate, when we feel overwhelmed by the magnitude of a problem, let us step back and recall the child, the widow, and the proverb. Let us remember also why the parable was told. The writer of Luke says that Jesus told this parable so his hearers would remember "to pray always and not to lose heart." Rather than pie-in-the-sky, this parable reminds us of God's goodness and justice that, unlike the frustrated judge's, are motivated by love.

Today we are the judge. The cries of the widow are the cries of mothers throughout our land and throughout the world. When will we listen? When will we grant justice? How long will it take to wear us down?

Today we are also the widow. We cry out for children — children of poverty, children at risk, children who are abused, children who are spoiled, children who are unwanted, children who have AIDS. Like the widow we must continue our pleading, for how else will the structures of power be worn down, as was the unjust judge?

As overwhelming as this may feel to us — finding ourselves both the widow and the judge — we persist because the parable, the proverb, and the child remind us that we can do nothing else. God is with us — when we succeed, and when we fail. God both calls us to this task and supports us in it.

Thus, we are judge and widow. When our task — whether to admit complicity and need of forgiveness or to stand strong for children — overwhelms us, we turn to God who forgives us and sustains us. We are filled with new resolve and return to our calling with hope and energy.

Questions for Reflection and Discussion
- When do you feel like the judge? When do you feel like the widow?
- What causes you to lose heart?
- What helps you to keep the faith or to persevere?

- Why is this parable important to persons and groups that seek justice? What does it teach you about God?
- How does this parable relate to the life and work of your committee, fellowship group, or congregation?

Prayer
Great God of justice and perseverance, grant us the gift of determination that we may wear down the walls of injustice and the footings that hold them up. Let us not lose heart, remembering that your love ever surrounds us. Call to us so that our prayers may be constant before you. Finally, keep us aware of the cries of children around us and throughout our world, so that we don't become the unjust judge. All this we ask in your great mercy and through Jesus the Christ. Amen.

Based on a reflection by Carol A. Wehrheim
Church Educator
Princeton, NJ

TOUCH THE WOUNDS

Focus: When we speak out for children, we confess our faith as we touch their wounds.

Scriptures: John 20:19-29

This gospel passage is commonly known as the story of Thomas the Doubter. Yet a more thoughtful exegesis might suggest that this disciple, who has wandered through nearly 2,000 years of church history with the epithet "doubting," got a bad rap.

Let's recall the scene. It was the night of a terrifying day, ending a week of awe and mystery. The tomb was empty; the women claimed to have seen Jesus; the town was in turmoil. The disciples — exhausted, confused, and terribly frightened — locked themselves in a room. In the midst of this tense meeting Jesus appeared and greeted them with peace. Thomas wasn't present, and he remained unconvinced when the others told him what had happened. A week later the disciples met again, and there, in their midst, appeared Jesus. Thomas still wasn't convinced, so Jesus invited Thomas to touch his wounds. Finally, in so doing, Thomas was persuaded that this man was their friend and teacher, Jesus. We have always seen this story as a tale of weak faith. Many of us were taught in childhood and beyond that we should aspire to be good and strong disciples, not doubting Thomases.

However, there is another way to look at this story. Perhaps Thomas was asking the relevant question for the men and women of his day and for us today: How will the world believe once the teacher, Jesus, is no longer with us? Doesn't our sad and doubting world ask the same question repeatedly? How are we to believe? How are those of us who neither knew Jesus personally nor witnessed his life and ministry firsthand to have faith?

It is in Jesus' response to Thomas that we may take solace and gain insight. Jesus responded to Thomas without hesitation and said, in effect, "If you would believe, then touch me here where the wounds fester. You would have faith? Then touch where the spear pierced my side or here, where the cruel nails were driven into my hands."

Perhaps Jesus would say the same to us today. How are we to believe? Reach out to the wounds and touch them. How are we to have faith? Put your fingers at that place where the body is wounded. This is quite a challenge in a time when our incapacity to touch has made AIDS patients pariahs and the homeless are pulled from city streets by hands covered with latex rubber gloves.

It is here, then, in this notion of acting in and on behalf of our own faith in the redemption of all humankind that we, like Thomas, must reach out and touch the wounds.

Most of us have difficulty touching wounds. In fact, we have to acknowledge that it is difficult enough for us to think about hungry or homeless children, let alone to touch them. Therefore, we must pray to God in the name of Jesus, whose gaze avoided no one and whose touch healed the sick, for the grace to overcome our reluctance, exploitation, and injustice.

We can touch the wounds inflicted by arrogance about race, class, gender, and ethnicity. We can touch the wounds of children without homes or schools or health care. We can touch the wounds of church policies and public policies that ignore the urgent needs of children. We can touch the wounds of families and communities broken by despair and poverty.

To touch such wounds is to stand with children. It is to include child advocacy in the larger mission of the church, precisely because it stands in the faith tradition of Jesus. As child advocates, to reach out and touch the wounds of the children of the world is to touch the wounds of our Savior, to remove doubts, to know faith.

Questions for Reflection and Discussion
- What new insights do you have into this Bible story?
- How have questions or doubts strengthened your faith?

- As you think about the children in your congregation and community, what are their wounds? What can you, your family, your committee, and your congregation do to touch these wounds?

Prayer

Holy One, Healer of all wounds, be with us as we search for faith to be your people. Help us see the wounds around us, especially those inflicted on children. Guide us to bring a healing touch of love and care, not given at a distance or hidden from view, but person to person. We pray all this in the name of Jesus Christ, whose gaze avoided no one and whose touch healed the sick. Amen.

Based on a sermon by the Rev. Eileen W. Lindner
Associate General Secretary for
Ecumenical Relations
National Council of Churches of Christ
New York, NY

RECEIVE THE STRANGER

Focus: When we welcome children in the name of Jesus, we welcome the God who created us.

Scripture: Mark 9:33-37

The two greatest sins for the people of Nepal are picking wildflowers and harming children. Disconcerting at first, the juxtaposition of these two acts calls attention to the fragile, seasonal beauty of children and our sacred duty to protect them. This Nepalese saying also contains a shocking truth: Children are more like wildflowers than they are like adult human beings. Children are not like us. This same truth underlies the story from Mark.

What makes this account in Mark so different from the other stories about Jesus and children is that it does not tell adults to *be* children or *become* like children in order to be part of the realm of God. Many sermons have focused on that idea, encouraging adults to be more playful, innocent, and open in order to be received into God's realm. Instead, this story says: If you want to be welcomed into the realm of God, you are to receive children as strangers and welcome them with a holy heart of gracious hospitality.

You are to receive children as strangers. Children, even our own, are strangers to us. We forget this, most of the time. We think we know all about them, better than they know themselves. We forget they are not like us when we confuse them with our younger selves and try to use them to make up for our own hurts, disappointments, or failures. We

forget they are not like us when we expect them to be miniature versions of adults, when we expect them to be well-behaved, always fitting into our world without muss or fuss.

The point of the story in Mark is that the world is not *our* world. Children are already welcome in it, and not only when they play by our rules. Instead, the world — the realm of God — is a world which we adults share with children, a world about which they teach us as much as we teach them. Certainly the same can be said about the faith community.

Here is the hard part: in order to learn from and with children what it means to be part of God's realm, we must accept that children are not like us. Because we were once children, we think we know all about childhood. We don't. Once we become adults, we forget what it is to *be* a child. The passage from childhood to adulthood is not like filling a balloon with air. It is more like changing from a caterpillar into a cocoon into a butterfly. It is a series of metamorphoses, of dramatic changes in which we leave behind forever our old life in order to take on a new one. As creative and hardworking as we may be in imagining and remembering our former selves as children, we cannot recapture what it is to *be* a child. So to experience the realm of God is not to *be* or *become* a child again. Rather, it is to come to know children, to receive them as strangers, to welcome them as the people of God — a people to which they already belong.

Questions for Reflection and Discussion
- How do you interpret the Nepalese saying? Could it be said about our nation? Why? Why not?
- What differences do you see between "becoming as a

child" and receiving or welcoming a child?

- How does this story from Mark and the commentary on it relate to your mission as a church? Your work as a committee? Your calling as a disciple of Jesus?

Prayer

To the One who welcomes all creation, we give praise. To the One who sent us a Son to show us the way, we give thanks. To the One who receives us even when we fail to acknowledge that acceptance, we ask forgiveness. To the One for whom no one is a stranger, we seek mercy. Now, as we go about our lives and our work together, send your Spirit to us that we may see you in our midst and always be ready to welcome Your presence in a child. In Jesus' name we pray. Amen.

Based on a sermon by Mary Potter Engel
Professor of Historical Theology
United Theological Seminary
Minneapolis, MN

SELLING THE SHADOW FOR THE SUBSTANCE: WHAT PARENTS AND THE COMMUNITY MUST DO FOR CHILDREN

Focus: We — each of us — are responsible for being role models and mentors for children — *all* children.

Scriptures: Proverbs 20:7
Proverbs 23:26

The wisdom of an illiterate slave woman, Sojourner Truth, has frequently guided me as I have struggled and continue to struggle to see, hear, understand, feel, and heal in my life. American parents, citizens, and leaders need to follow Sojourner's advice "to sell the shadow to support the substance," to be able to know the difference between them, and to pass on that understanding to our children. My parents, many other "ordinary" black adults, and black leaders taught these lessons to my generation of black children.

As the granddaughter, daughter, and sister of Baptist ministers, service was as essential a part of my upbringing as eating and sleeping and going to school. The church was a hub of black children's social existence, and caring black adults were buffers against the segregated prison of the outside world that told us we were inferior and unimportant. But our parents said it wasn't so. Our teachers said it wasn't so. And our preachers said it wasn't so. So the message I internalized, despite the ugly racism of my childhood, was to let no man or woman look down on you and to look down on no man or woman.

Children were taught, not by sermonizing but by personal example, that nothing was too lowly to do, and that the work of our hands and the work of our minds were of equal dignity and value. I remember a debate my parents had about whether I was too young to go with an older brother to help clean the bed and bedsores of a very sick, poor woman. I went. And I'm grateful. I learned early how much even the smallest helping hand can mean to a lonely, suffering person.

I also was taught not to ask in the face of need, "Why doesn't somebody do something?" but rather, "Why don't I do something?" As black children, we couldn't play in public playgrounds or sit at drugstore counters and order a Coke, so my Daddy built a playground and canteen behind the church. Whenever he saw a need, he tried to respond. There were no homes for the black aged in South Carolina so he began one across the street, and he and my mother and we children cooked and served and cleaned. I resented it sometimes, but I learned that it was my responsibility to take care of elderly family members and neighbors, and that everybody was my neighbor. My mother carried on "the old folks' home" after my father died, and one of my brothers has carried it on since our mother died in 1984.

Finding another child in my room or a pair of my shoes gone was far from unusual, and 12 foster children followed my sister and me and my three brothers as we left home. When my mother died, an old white man in my town asked me what I did. In a flash I realized I do exactly what my parents did — just on a different scale. The ugly external voices of assault of my rural segregated childhood (as a very young child I remember standing and hearing former South Carolina Sen. James Byrnes railing at the local courthouse) were tempered by the internal voices of parental and community expectation and pride. My father and I waited anxiously for the *Brown v. Board of Education* decision. We talked about it and what it would mean for my future and the future of millions of other black children. He died the week before *Brown* was decided. But I and other children lucky enough to have caring and courageous parents were able, in later years, to walk through the new but heavy doors that *Brown* slowly and painfully opened. I remember Langston Hughes coming to my small town, reading poetry and signing a book of poems I still treasure. And I remember having dinner at Benedict College in Columbia, South Carolina, with Mary McLeod Bethune, founder of the National Council of Negro Women, and hearing her boast, "The blacker the berry, the sweeter the juice!", and her stories about going into segregated shops to buy hats and overwhelming the flabbergasted white sales clerks with, "Do you know who I am? I am Mary McLeod Bethune!"

Caring black adults at all levels, within and without my family, countered the constant negative messages of the outside world. Child-rearing and parental work were inseparable. I went everywhere with my parents and was under the watchful eyes of members of the congregation and community who were my extended parents. They kept me when my parents went out of town, they reported on and chided me when I strayed from the straight and narrow of community expectations, and they basked in and supported my achievements when I did well. Doing well meant high academic achievement, playing the piano for Sunday school or singing, participating in church activities, being helpful to somebody, displaying good manners (which is nothing more than consideration toward others), and reading. I was reminded recently that the only time my Daddy would not give us a chore ("Can't you find something constructive to do?" was his favorite refrain, and he always made sure we did have something constructive to do) was when we were reading. So we read a lot and were clear early on about what our parents and extended community parents valued.

My brother Harry, at a 1981 tribute to our mother by the Mothers Club of the Shiloh Baptist Church (which she founded), thanked her for providing us three things that he thought were instrumental in helping all of us set and reach individual goals: elementary courtesy, character, and respect; inspiring us to dream; and leading us to an awareness of the reality of God.

"Throughout our lives," he said, "we shall reflect your teaching, and you shall live as long as we shall live." And, I hope, as long as our children and their children and their children's children shall live.

Black adults in our churches and community made children feel valued and valuable. They took time and paid attention to us. They struggled to find ways to keep us busy. While life often was very hard and resources very scarce, as it is for so many today, we always knew who we were, and that the measure of our worth was inside our heads and hearts and not on our backs or in other people's minds. We were told that the world had a lot of problems, that black people had extra problems, but that we were able and obligated to struggle and change them; that being poor or black was no excuse for not achieving; and that extra intellectual and material gifts brought with them the privilege and responsibility of sharing with others less fortunate. As a result we never lost hope, like so many children have today. We learned that service is the rent we pay for living. It is the very purpose of life, not something you do in your spare time. And nobody ever promised that it would be simple or easy.

The legacies my parents and preachers and teachers left to my generation of black children were priceless, but not material: a living faith reflected in daily service, the discipline of hard work and stick-to-it-ness, and a capacity to struggle in the face of adversity ("giving up" and "burnout" were not part of the language of my elders — you got up every morning and you did what you had to do and you got up every time you fell down and tried as many times as you had to until you got it done right). They had grit. They valued family life and family rituals, and tried to expose us to good role models.

Role models were of two kinds: those who achieved in the outside world like Marian Anderson, my namesake; former Morehouse College president and Martin Luther King, Jr.'s mentor Benjamin Mays; and former Howard University President Mordecai Johnson, whose three- and four-hour speeches I sat through once a year (my parents believed in osmosis!) even before I could understand or stay awake through them; and those who didn't have a whole lot of education or fancy clothes but who taught us, by the special grace of their lives and without ever opening a book on philosophy or theology other than the Bible, that the kingdom of God is within — in what you are, not in what you have or look like. And I still hope I can be half as good as Miz Lucy McQueen, Miz Tee Kelly, Miz Kate Winston, and Miz Amie Byers (who helped me raise my three sons), "uneducated" but very wise and smart women, who were kind and patient and loving with children and with others. When I went to Spelman College, Miz Tee sent me shoe boxes with chicken and biscuits and greasy dollar bills. And I think you and I owe our children and their children the same kind of loving support as was given to us by these and so many others like them, of every race and class in America, on whose shoulders of sacrifice and care we all stand today.

It never occurred to any Wright child we were not going to college or were not expected to share what we learned with the less fortunate. I was 40 years old before I figured out that when my Daddy often responded to my requests for money by saying he didn't have any change, he meant he *really* didn't have any, rather than meaning "nothing smaller than a $20 bill." When he died, in 1954, he had holes in his shoes but two children out of college, a child in college, and another in divinity school. He knew the difference between substance and shadow.

Questions for Reflection and Discussion
- Who are the persons who showed you substance when you were growing up? How do you feel when you recall them?
- The verses from the book of Proverbs are just two of many that remind us of the connections between chil-

dren and adults and the attainment of wisdom, or the giving of substance rather than shadow. Look through this section for others. What insights about relating to children do they give you?

- In the meditation parents are important figures, but so too are many other adults, related and unrelated. How does your congregation encourage adults to provide substance for children outside their family or outside your congregation?
- What roles of leadership might your board or committee take to see that all children are provided with a variety of role models, and to support families in the task of nurturing?

Prayer

God of Grace, who created us to be in community with one another and with you, hold us closely as we strain to know the difference between substance and shadow in your sight. Open our eyes and unplug our ears that we may know true wisdom. Alert us to integrity of word and deed. Then grant us the courage and perseverance both to say and do that which is wise and righteous in the presence of children. In Jesus' name, we pray. Amen.

A reflection written by Marian Wright Edelman
President
Children's Defense Fund
Washington, DC

TWO MEDITATIONS FOR THE HOLIDAY SEASON

THE HOPE OF A CHILD

Focus: Advent is the season of hope and expectancy; all children deserve to be a part of this hope and assured of their survival.

Scripture: Luke 1:46-50

Each December wide eyed and expectant children all over the world wait for Christmas. They wait for presents, to see Grandma and Grandpa, to visit Santa, or to be a lamb or angel in the Christmas pageant. Children also wait to celebrate the birth of the Christ child, the Savior who came with a promise to change the bitterness of a world living without reconciliation. Their eyes reflect the expectancy and hope that is the essence of the Advent season. With each day, the expectancy builds as they dream of what Christmas Day will hold for them. The prophet Isaiah told the people of God what Christmas Day would hold — the coming of One who is called Wonderful Counselor, Mighty God, Everlasting Father, Prince of Peace.

Parents awaiting the arrival of their first child are full of dreams, too. They imagine the kind of life their child will lead. They want the child to enjoy brightly lighted Christmas trees, and to know the love of God. They want their child never to be cold or hungry. During the Christmas season, many children and their families are waiting for something good which they hope will come.

During this time of Advent and through all the seasons of the year there are families who are waiting for something good which may never come. Nearly one-fifth of all children in the United States are poor, and one-third of all poor children are not covered by health insurance. How can they declare God's mercy from generation to generation?

Only children who have an even chance of survival can dream the visions of the Christmas to come. Only children for whom those dreams come true, at least once in a while, can approach Advent with the compassion and expectancy that we learn from Isaiah. Only children who know themselves to be lovingly nurtured and nourished can recognize the loving presence of God through a baby born into poverty nearly 2,000 years ago. Only we can make the dream of survival a reality for all. God grant us that courage.

Questions for Reflection and Discussion
- What hopes or dreams do you hear from the children you know? How are these related to the hope we celebrate during Advent?
- Who are the children without hope in your community? How can you minister to and with them?
- What role does your congregation or committee have in bringing hope to children in your congregation? In your community? In this nation? In the world?

Prayer
Almighty God, Giver of Hope, praised be your name. Provide us with the courage and stamina to be bearers of hope to the children of your world, even when we are without hope. Grant us the newness of faith that we may be filled with the hope Isaiah brought to the nation of Israel. Show us the great light that we may rejoice before you. In the name of the Messiah who is to come. Amen.

THE HEART OF A CHILD

Focus   We can turn a child's heart to God when we reveal God and emulate Christ through loving and empowering relationships with children.

Scripture: Luke 1:51-55

After the weeks of preparation during Advent, Christmas arrives and we open our hearts to celebrate the birth of Jesus Christ. We celebrate not because of the birth of Jesus Christ as a baby, even though the message of the heavenly host and the visit of the Magi mark this birth as an extraordinary one. We celebrate this birth because of who the baby has become in our lives — the Savior, the fulfillment of the promise to the people of Israel, and to all their descendants.

Christ came that our hearts and the hearts of children everywhere might be filled with love, not hate; with hope, not despair; with compassion, not selfishness. Christ came to change the hearts of humankind in that ancient time and today. Christ came to teach all creation how to love God and one another.

How we love our children has a powerful influence on how they will love others, and God. How we love others, seen and unseen, teaches our children our understanding of the love Christ has brought to us. What kind of love do we give our children? What kind of love do we teach by example? We can strive to love children as unconditionally as God loves us. We can give to others as wholly as Christ gave for us. We can speak out for children in places of power as courageously as Christ spoke out for children and all those who were powerless. We can welcome children into our midst as Christ beckoned them to him. When we do all this in the example of Christ, we help shape the hearts of our children, and reshape our own as well.

Question for Reflection and Discussion

- Who are the powerless children in your congregation? In your community? In your nation?
- How can you, your family, your committee, and your congregation represent these children to those in the seats of power?
- What examples do your children see of God's love in your congregation? How can your committee make these examples more visible to children? How can your committee increase the examples for children to see and participate in?

Prayer

Loving God, Shaper of the universe and Bestower of all good things, when we pause to ponder your love we know that we can never comprehend its breadth or its depth. May we daily show our children but glimpses of that love so they too will give their hearts to you. Teach us to stand up to evil and to speak for children and all others who are powerless in the sight of our ruler. For us we pray. Amen.

Based on a biblical reflection by the Rev. Ruth Fowler
Pastor
Richboro Baptist Church
Staten Island, NY

CHAPTER 2

CHILDREN AND THE BIBLE

The verses and passages here are from the *New Revised Standard Version* of the Bible. Read through them for an overview of the biblical basis for ministry with and for children. Use them for personal reflection as the basis of a sermon or Bible study, to prepare a litany, as verses for banners or posters, or to combine them in a choral reading. All of the biblical passages cited in Chapter 1 of this section are found here.

Then Esau said, "Let us journey on our way, and I will go alongside you." But Jacob said to him, "My lord knows that the children are frail and that the flocks and herds, which are nursing, are a care to me; and if they are overdriven for one day, all the flocks will die. Let my lord pass on ahead of his servant, and I will lead on slowly, according to the pace of the cattle that are before me and according to the pace of the children, until I come to my lord in Seir."

Genesis 33:12-14

You shall not wrong or oppress a resident alien, for you were aliens in the land of Egypt. You shall not abuse any widow or orphan. If you do abuse them, when they cry out to me, I will surely heed their cry....

Exodus 22:21-23

Hear, O Israel: The Lord is our God, the Lord alone. You shall love the Lord your God with all your heart, and with all your soul, and with all your might. Keep these words that I am commanding you today in your heart. Recite them to your children and talk about them when you are at home and when you are away, when you lie down and when you rise. Bind them as a sign on your hand, fix them as an emblem on your forehead, and write them on the doorposts of your house and on your gates.

Deuteronomy 6:4-9

O Lord, you will hear the desire of the meek; you will strengthen their heart, you will incline your ear to do justice for the orphan and the oppressed, so that those from earth may strike terror no more.

Psalm 10:17-18

Yet it was you who took me from the womb, you kept me safe on my mother's breast. On you I was cast from my birth, and since my mother bore me you have been my God. Do not be far from me, for trouble is near and there is no one to help.

Psalm 22:9-11

Father of orphans and protector of widows is God in his holy habitation. God gives the desolate a home to live in; he leads out the prisoners to prosperity, but the rebellious live in a parched land.

Psalm 68:5-6

Happy is everyone who fears the Lord, who walks in his ways. You shall eat the fruit of the labor of your hands; you shall be happy, and it shall go well with you. Your wife will be like a fruitful vine within your house; your children will be like olive shoots around your table. Thus shall the man be blessed who fears the Lord. The Lord bless you from Zion. May you see the prosperity of Jerusalem all the days of your life. May you see your children's children. Peace be upon Israel!

Psalm 128

O Lord, my heart is not lifted up, my eyes are not raised too high; I do not occupy myself with things too great and too marvelous for me. But I have calmed and quieted my soul, like a weaned child with its mother; my soul is like the weaned child that is with me. O Israel, hope in the Lord from this time on and forevermore.

Psalm 131

May our sons in their youth be like plants full grown, our daughters like corner pillars, cut for the building of a palace.

Psalm 144:12

The righteous walk in integrity — happy are the children who follow them!

Proverbs 20:7

Train children in the right way, and when old, they will not stray.

Proverbs 22:6

My child, give me your heart, and let your eyes observe my ways.

Proverbs 23:26

Speak out for those who cannot speak, for the rights of all the destitute. Speak out, judge righteously, defend the rights of the poor and needy.

Proverbs 31:8-9

For a child has been born for us, a son given to us; authority rests upon his shoulders; and he is named Wonderful Counselor, Mighty God, Everlasting Father, Prince of Peace.

Isaiah 9:6

A shoot shall come out from the stump of Jesse, and a branch shall grow out of his roots.... His delight shall be in the fear of the Lord. He shall not judge by what his eyes see, or decide by what his ears hear; but with righteousness he shall judge the poor, and decide with equity for the meek of the earth.... The wolf shall live with the lamb, the leopard shall lie down with the kid, the calf and the lion and the fatling together, and a little child shall lead them.

Isaiah 11:1, 3-4, 6

Is not this the fast that I choose: to loose the bonds of injustice, to undo the thongs of the yoke, to let the oppressed go free, and to break every yoke? Is it not to share your bread with the hungry, and bring the homeless poor into your house; when you see the naked, to cover them, and not to hide yourself from your own kin? Then your light shall break forth like the dawn, and your healing shall spring up quickly; your vindicator shall go before you, the glory of the Lord shall be your rear guard. Then you shall call, and the Lord will answer; you shall cry for help, and he will say, Here I am.

Isaiah 58:6-9a

And the streets of the city shall be full of boys and girls playing in its streets.

Zechariah 8:5

When Herod saw that he had been tricked by the wise men, he was infuriated, and he sent and killed all the children in and around Bethlehem who were two years old or under, according to the time that he had learned from the wise men. Then was fulfilled what had been spoken through the prophet Jeremiah:

"A voice was heard in Ramah, wailing and loud lamentation, Rachel weeping for her children; she refused to be consoled, because they are no more."

Matthew 2:16-18

"Ask, and it will be given you; search, and you will find; knock, and the door will be opened for you. For everyone who asks receives, and everyone who searches finds, and for everyone who knocks, the door will be opened. Is there anyone among you who, if your child asks for bread, will give a stone? Or if the child asks for a fish, will give a snake? If you then, who are evil, know how to give good gifts to your children, how much more will your Father in heaven give good things to those who ask him!"

Matthew 7:7-11

At that time the disciples came to Jesus and asked, "Who is the greatest in the kingdom of heaven?" He called a child, whom he put among them, and said, "Truly I tell you, unless you change and become like children, you will never enter the kingdom of heaven. Whoever becomes humble like this child is the greatest in the kingdom of heaven. Whoever welcomes one such child in my name welcomes me.

"If any of you put a stumbling block before one of these little ones who believe in me, it would be better for you if a great millstone were fastened around your neck and you were drowned in the depth of the sea. Woe to the world because of stumbling blocks! Occasions for stumbling are bound to come, but woe to the one by whom the stumbling block comes!"

Matthew 18:1-7
See also Mark 9:33-37, 42 and
Luke 9:46-48

"Teacher, which commandment in the law is the greatest?" [Jesus] said to him, "'You shall love the Lord your God with all your heart, and with all your soul, and with all your mind.' This is the greatest and first commandment. And a second is like it: 'You shall love your neighbor as yourself.' On these two commandments hang all the law and the prophets."

Matthew 22:36-40

People were bringing little children to him in order that he might touch them; and the disciples spoke sternly to them. But when Jesus saw this, he was indignant and said to them, "Let the little children come to me; do not stop them;

for it is to such as these that the kingdom of God belongs. Truly I tell you, whoever does not receive the kingdom of God as a little child will never enter it." And he took them up in his arms, laid his hands on them, and blessed them.

Mark 10:13-16
See also Matthew 19:13-15 and
Luke 18:15-17

And Mary said, "My soul magnifies the Lord, and my spirit rejoices in God my Savior, for he has looked with favor on the lowliness of his servant. Surely, from now on all generations will call me blessed; for the Mighty One has done great things for me, and holy is his name. His mercy is for those who fear him from generation to generation. He has shown strength with his arm; he has scattered the proud in the thoughts of their hearts. He has brought down the powerful from their thrones, and lifted up the lowly; he has filled the hungry with good things, and sent the rich away empty. He has helped his servant Israel, in remembrance of his mercy, according to the promise he made to our ancestors, to Abraham and to his descendants forever."

Luke 1:46-55

Then Jesus told them a parable about their need to pray always and not to lose heart. He said, "In a certain city there was a judge who neither feared God nor had respect for people. In that city there was a widow who kept coming to him and saying, `Grant me justice against my opponent.' For a while he refused; but later he said to himself, `Though I have no fear of God and no respect for anyone, yet because this widow keeps bothering me, I will grant her justice, so that she may not wear me out by continually coming....'" And the Lord said, "Listen to what the unjust judge says. And will not God grant justice to his chosen ones who cry to him day and night? Will he delay long in helping them? I tell you, he will quickly grant justice to them. And yet, when the Son of Man comes, will he find faith on earth?"

Luke 18:1-8

After this Jesus went to the other side of the Sea of Galilee, also called the Sea of Tiberias. A large crowd kept following him, because they saw the signs that he was doing for the sick. Jesus went up the mountain and sat down there with his disciples. Now the Passover, the festival of the Jews, was near. When he looked up and saw a large crowd coming toward him, Jesus said to Philip, "Where are we to buy bread for these people to eat?" He said this to test him, for he himself knew what he was going to do. Philip answered him, "Six months' wages would not buy enough bread for each of them to get a little." One of his disciples, Andrew, Simon Peter's brother, said to him, "There is a boy here who has five barley loaves and two fish. But what are they among so many people?" Jesus said, "Make the people sit down." Now there was a great deal of grass in the place; so they sat down, about five thousand in all. Then Jesus took the loaves, and when he had given thanks, he distributed them to those who were seated; so also the fish, as much as they wanted. When they were satisfied, he told his disciples, "Gather up the fragments left over, so that nothing may be lost." So they gathered them up, and from the fragments of the five barley loaves, left by those who had eaten, they filled twelve baskets. When the people saw the sign that he had done, they began to say, "This is indeed the prophet who is to come into the world."

John 6:1-14

But Thomas (who was called the Twin), one of the twelve, was not with [the disciples] when Jesus came. So the other disciples told him, "We have seen the Lord." But he said to them, "Unless I see the mark of the nails in his hands, and put my finger in the mark of the nails and my hand in his side, I will not believe."

A week later his disciples were again in the house, and Thomas was with them. Although the doors were shut, Jesus came and stood among them and said, "Peace be with you." Then he said to Thomas, "Put your finger here and see my hands. Reach out your hand and put it in my side. Do not doubt but believe." Thomas answered him, "My Lord and my God!" Jesus said to him, "Have you believed because you have seen me? Blessed are those who have not seen and yet have come to believe."

John 20:24-29

Let mutual love continue. Do not neglect to show hospitality to strangers, for by doing that some have entertained angels without knowing it. Remember those who are in prison, as though you were in prison with them; those who are being tortured, as though you yourselves were being tortured.

Hebrews 13:1-3

CHAPTER 3

PRAYERS, LITANIES, POEMS, STORIES, AND SONGS

PRAYERS AND LITANIES

The prayers and litanies in this section are samples for you to use as you find them, to adapt, or to use as models in preparing your own. For the litanies, the leader's words are in regular type, and the people's response in **boldface**.

Call to Worship

Leader: Let us praise God who has brought us together.

All: **With one voice we give praise.**

Leader: Dear friends, the gift of children is both a joyous and a solemn treasure with which we have been entrusted. We are gathered together today to celebrate and to honor children and to remind ourselves of our responsibility to them. It is an occasion for rejoicing and for remembrance. Let us join in giving thanks to God, the Giver of life, for the gift of children; and raise our voices, together in prayer, for our children's many needs.

*From Recognizing and Celebrating Children
Congregations Concerned for Children
Minneapolis, MN*

Prayer of Confession (in unison)

God, forgive us for being asleep so often when you need us. You writhe in the agony of the world's hungry, while we worry over the menu. You weep with the soul of one who is friendless, while we fret over whom to invite to some social occasion. God, forgive us for sometimes taking our children, your children, for granted, and not hearing their special needs, for not loving them as you require. Wake us up to the needs of our sisters and brothers everywhere. In Christ's name we pray. Amen.

Assurance of Forgiveness

"The mercy of God is everlasting." Such is the witness of our heritage, which, being interpreted for our times, means: Now and in every moment our every past is accepted, our future is opened, our every present is offered to us afresh. This is the truth that sets us free. In Jesus Christ we are forgiven and set free. Amen.

*Written for the closing service of worship for the
Child Advocacy Conference
Presbyterian Church (USA)
Tampa, FL*

A Litany for Children

O Lord of light and Source of all creation, we praise and glorify you for the children you have given us.

Accept our thanksgiving, O Lord.

For their lives, their inquiring minds and receptive spirits, for their health and growth,

We humbly praise you, O God.

For their beauty and innocence, their laughter and tears, their joyous ways that fill us with wonder and delight,

We humbly praise you, O God.

For their youthful vision by which you lead them trustingly into the future,

We humbly praise you, O God.

For your constant protection which keeps them safe from harm,

We humbly praise you, O God.

For our families and for your loving forgiveness which allows parents and children to make mistakes and, confessing them, to continue to live in harmony,

We humbly praise you, O God.

O God of Abraham, Isaac, Jacob, of Sarah, Rachel, and Rebecca, of your prophets and teachers in every time and place, generation after generation you call your children forth to honor and obey you.

In awe and gratitude we praise you, O Lord.

For our children's growth in faith and their simple trust in you in these complex and troubled times,

We thank you, O Lord.

That your Spirit will remain with them as they grow, guiding them in the ways of justice, righteousness, and peace,

We pray to you, O Lord.

For all those who in the faith minister to and teach our children and are models of truth and goodness,

We thank you, O Lord.

* * *

Defender of the oppressed and the orphan, we pray for all children in our nation and our world who suffer from poverty, injustice, and fear.

Hear the cries of your children, O Lord.

For children who are runaways, homeless, in institutions, or jails,

In your tender mercy, protect them, God.

For children who are disabled in mind or body,

In your tender mercy, encourage and strengthen them, O God.

For children who this day will not have enough to eat,

In your tender mercy, provide them food, O God.

For babies born at risk, for children who are sick, and for those who lack proper health care, especially pregnant teenagers,

In your tender mercy, help and sustain them, O God.

For children who are victims of race or class discrimination, poor education, drug or alcohol abuse, and hopelessness,

In your tender mercy, grant them lives of hope and a future, O God.

For children who daily experience the fear and pain of war and civil strife, especially the child of _____,

In your tender mercy, defend and protect them, O God.

* * *

O God, Loving Parent, we pray for our families and the families of our nation,

Open our hearts, O Lord.

For children and parents forced to live apart because of poverty, illness, jail sentences, or migratory work,

Embrace and uphold them, Spirit of God.

For children and parents enduring the pain and grief of death or divorce,

Send your comfort, Spirit of God.

For families facing loss of jobs or the anxiety of an uncertain future,

Give them hope, Spirit of God.

For children and parents who live in conflict and misunderstanding,

Give them your peace and truth, Spirit of God.

For single mothers and single fathers who experience the burden of raising children alone,

Grant them courage and love, Spirit of God.

* * *

O Ruler of all, our sure defense, we pray for the world our children live in and will inherit.

Have pity on us, O Lord.

For the sake of all children, bring an end to the buildup and proliferation of nuclear weapons. Preserve us from attitudes and acts that threaten the annihilation of all life and the future we hold in trust for the children.

We cry to you, Creator of all.

For the sake of all children, bring an end to conflict and war between nations. Give us hearts and minds of peace and help us to teach peace to our children.

We cry to you, Creator of all.

For the sake of all children, bring an end to our misuse and pollution of the land, air, and water of the Earth. Teach us to be stewards and guardians of your creation.

We cry to you, Creator of all.

For the sake of all children, bring an end to the injustices caused and abetted by those in places of power. May our hearts and minds be changed by the cries of your hungry and suffering children.

We cry to you, Creator of all.

* * *

O Holy God, through whom all things are transformed and made whole, grant us and our children newness of life. Refresh and sustain us with the glorious vision of your world to come in which all children will live in peace and harmony, all children will be filled with good things to eat, and all children will rest secure in your love.

O God Most High, whom we name Yahweh, Lord, and Our Father, Creator, Redeemer, and Sanctifier of the world, we ask these things on behalf of our children and generations yet unborn who will live to praise your Holy Name, world without end. Amen.

Written by the Children's Defense Fund for National Children's Day, June 1982 The Washington Cathedral Washington, DC

Benediction

Into your hands, O God, we place ourselves, the guardians of your children. Support and strengthen us as we seek to make the world a more welcoming place for them. Unify us in our concern and respect for them.

Into your hands also we place the children of our homes, our cities, and the world. Support them in their joys and in their sorrows, strengthen their families, enlighten their governments, shelter them from evil, and, through your guidance, may we respond to their needs that they may discover the joy of your creation and know the bounty of your unending love. All this we ask in your name. Amen.

From Recognizing and Celebrating Children Congregations Concerned for Children Minneapolis, MN

POEMS

Greenless Child

I watched her go uncelebrated into the second grade,
A greenless child,
Gray among the orange and yellow,
Attached too much to corners and to other people's sunshine.
She colors the rainbow brown
And leaves balloons unopened in their packages.
Oh who will touch this greenless child?
Who will plant alleluias in her heart
And send her dancing into all the colors of God?
Or will she be left like an unwrapped package on the kitchen
    table —
Too dull for anyone to take the trouble?
Does God think we're her keeper?

Ann Weems, from Reaching for Rainbows: Resources from Creative Worship *Copyright 1980, The Westminster Press Reprinted and used by permission of The Westminster/John Knox Press*

The Cry of the Children

Do ye hear the children weeping, O my brothers,
Ere the sorrow comes with years?
They are leaning their young heads against their mothers,
And *that* cannot stop their tears.
The young lambs are bleating in the meadows,
The young birds are chirping in the nest,
The young fawns are playing with the shadows,
The young flowers are blowing toward the west —
But the young, young children, O my brothers,

They are weeping bitterly!
They are weeping in the playtime of the others,
In the country of the free.

Elizabeth Barrett Browning (1843)

Children Learn What They Live

If children live with criticism, they learn to condemn.
If children live with hostility, they learn to fight.
If children live with ridicule, they learn to be shy.
If children live with shame, they learn to feel guilty.
If children live with tolerance, they learn to be patient.
If children live with encouragement, they learn confidence.
If children live with praise, they learn to appreciate.
If children live with fairness, they learn justice.
If children live with security, they learn to have faith.
If children live with approval, they learn to like themselves.
If children live with acceptance and friendship, they learn to
    find love in the world.

Adapted from Dorothy Law Nolte Baptist Leader July 1972

A Child

Bitter are the tears of a child: sweeten them.
Deep are the thoughts of a child: quiet them.
Sharp is the grief of a child: take it from him.
Soft is the heart of a child: do not harden it.

Lady Pamela Wyndham Glenconner (Nineteenth century)

The Child's Name Is "Today"

We are guilty of many errors and faults but our
worst crime is abandoning the children,
neglecting the fountain of life.
Many of the things we need can wait. The
child cannot.

Right now is the time bones are being formed,
blood is being made, senses are being developed.
To the child we cannot answer "Tomorrow."
The child's name is "Today."

Adapted from a poem by Gabriela Mistral
Nobel Prize-winning poet from Chile

Stories

The Story of the Children's Fire

The whole community sits around a circle called a Medicine
Wheel. Around that wheel are representatives of all the
different aspects of the community. In the East, there's the
fool. In the West, there's the witch. In the South, there's the
hunter. In the North, there's the creator. Others positioned
around the circle are the shaman, the politician, etc. And in
the center of the circle is the children's fire. Next to the
children's fire sit the grandfather and grandmother. If you
want to build a condominium in the community of Spirit
Lake, you have to enter the Medicine Wheel in the East, at
the position of the fool. The question you ask is, "May I
build a condo on Spirit Lake?" The fool takes your question,
turns it around backwards and asks, "What would Spirit
Lake say about such a condo?" You then have to take the
question the fool gives you to everyone around the Medicine
Wheel. Each will respond to you according to their position
in the community. The last people you must ask the question
to are the grandmother and grandfather who guard the
children's fire. If these two decide that the request is not
good for the children's fire, then the answer is "no." They
are the only ones in the circle who have veto power. The
concept of the ultimate question is simple. Does it hurt or
help the children's fire? If it can pass the test of the children's
fire, then it can be done.

Excerpted from materials by Congregations Concerned
for Children.
(This story was told to Magaly Rodriguez Mossman by
Robin Van Doren, who heard it from elders of the Hopi
Nation.)

For Their Sake

When Israel stood to receive the Torah,
The Holy One, blessed be He, said to them:
I am giving you my Torah. Bring me good guarantors
that you will guard it, and I shall give it to
you.
They said: Our fathers are our guarantors.
The Holy One, blessed be He, said to them:

Your fathers are unacceptable to me.
Yet bring me good guarantors, and I shall give it
to you.
They said to him:
Master of the Universe, our prophets are
our guarantors.
He said to them:
Your prophets are unacceptable to me.
Yet bring me good guarantors, and I shall
give it to you.
Behold, our children are our guarantors.
The Holy One, blessed be He, said:
They are certainly good guarantors.
For their sake, I give you the Torah.

Canticles Rabbah (Midrash)

A Ten-Year-Old's Story

I was asked to tell you what it's like to live in a single-parent
home with no money.

Sometimes it's sad because I feel different from other
kids. For instance, when other kids get to go to fun places
and I can't because I don't have enough money and they do.

Most of my friends get an allowance but I don't because
my mom doesn't have enough money to pay me. They get to
get the things that they want and need and I don't.

The other day in school we had this balloon contest, and
it only cost one dollar and out of three years I haven't been
able to get one.

Me and my brother are a little hard on shoes. This summer the only shoes we had were thongs and when church
time came, the only shoes we had to wear were one pair of
church shoes. The one that got them first got to wear them.
The one that didn't had to wear a pair of my mom's tennis
shoes or my sister's.

I have a big brother. He is not my real brother. He is
with the Big Brothers and Big Sisters Association. Once I
tried to tell my big brother about welfare. It was so embarrassing I was about to cry. I don't like Joe just because he
takes me to a fun place every week; I like Joe because he
makes me feel special.

Sometimes I pray that I won't be poor no more and sometimes I sit up at night and cry. But it didn't change anything. Crying just helps the hurt and the pain. It doesn't change anything.

One day, I asked my mom why the kids always tease me and she said because they don't understand, but I do understand about being on welfare and being poor, and it can hurt.

An anonymous 10-year-old

HYMNS, SONGS, AND ANTHEMS

All Things Bright and Beautiful by C.F. Alexander
Children of the Heavenly Father (traditional Swedish song)
Help O Lord by Bob Russ and John Ylvisaker
Love Them Now by Richard Avery and Donald Marsh
Live Into Hope by Jane Parker Huber
Help Us Accept Each Other by Fred Kaan and Doreen Potter
O God of All the Years of Life by Jane Parker Huber
Hope for the Children by Douglas Clark
If We're Going to Walk Together by R. Tiffany Bates
We Thank You, God, for Strength of Arm by Robert Davis
*He's Got the Whole World in His Hands**
Jesus Loves Me by Anna Warner*
Kumbaya (traditional)*
The Lord of the Dance by Sydney Carter*
Morning Has Broken by Eleanor Farjeon*
Pass It On (Replace "friend" in verse 3 with "child") by Kurt Kaiser*
The Prayer of St. Francis (Make Me a Channel of Your Peace) music by Sebastian Temple*
Seek Ye First by Karen Lafferty*
We Shall Overcome by Frank Hamilton, Guy Carawan, Zilpia Horton, and Pete Seeger*
Child of Wonder by Marty Haugen**

* In *Songs*, compiled by Yohann Anderson. Tunebook ($21.95 plus shipping and handling) available from: Songs and Creations, Inc., P.O. Box 7, San Anselmo, CA 94960. Tel: 1-800-227-2188.
** GIA Publications, 7404 South Mason Avenue, Chicago, IL 60638.

Prayer for Change
Tune: Dix: *For the Beauty of the Earth*
(Refrain changes words)

1. For the beauty of the earth,
   For the glory of the skies,
   For the children ev'rywhere,
   With their sad or joyful cries,
   God of All, to Thee we raise
   This our hymn of grateful praise.
2. For the beauty of the earth,
   For the glory of the skies,
   For each child whose life of worth
   May be missed by human eyes,
   God of All, to Thee we raise
   This our hymn of grateful praise.
3. For the hungry, homeless ones
   Seeking life despite despair,
   For the nations buying guns
   While the children wait for care,
   God of all, this plea we raise:
   Help us change our hurtful ways.
4. Thanks for gifts the children bring:
   Love and trust and open hands.
   Help us give them songs to sing,
   Meet their needs as love commands.
   God of all, this prayer we raise:
   Let us bring forth better days.

Virginia Sargent
American Baptist Churches in the U.S.A.

CHAPTER 4

ORGANIZING A CHILDREN'S DAY AND CHILDREN'S SABBATH

HISTORY OF CHILDREN'S DAY

The first Children's Day in the United States was celebrated in June 1856 at the Universalist Church in Chelsea, Massachusetts. It followed the European tradition of Confirmation Day in the Roman Catholic and Lutheran churches, when all the children of the congregation carried bouquets of spring flowers into the church. By 1868 Children's Day was recognized officially by the Methodist Church as the second Sunday in June, and soon other denominations began observing it. Children's Day is now part of the calendar of the National Council of Churches. (From *Days and Customs of All Faiths*, Fleet, 1957.)

CHILDREN'S SABBATH DAY IN YOUR CHURCH

For some congregations, a Children's Sabbath Day (also known as Rally Day) is already an annual tradition. For others, it may be a new worship and fellowship experience. Whatever your congregation's situation, use this occasion to celebrate children as an integral part of your faith community, to raise awareness about the issues affecting children, especially those in need, and to involve all ages of the congregation in activities that both celebrate children and help meet their needs.

PLANNING A CHILDREN'S SABBATH DAY

Considering a Theme and Format

As you think about planning this special day, use one of the meditations from pages 11-20 and reflect on the importance of children in your life and in the life of your community of faith. Jesus often pointed to children as models for our spiritual development. They are the source of our hope for the future. Their care and welfare is the responsibility of every adult Christian.

The theme of a Children's Sabbath Day can focus on the role that children have in the life of your congregation and the potential they have for greater participation. A Children's Sabbath can introduce a specific scriptural theme, such as "Let the Children Come to Me." A Children's Sabbath can inform and involve the congregation in a social issue especially pertinent to the children in your local area, whether that be child poverty or adoption and foster care.

Once you have reflected on and selected a possible theme for the Children's Sabbath Day, you may want to give some preliminary consideration to the potential scope or format of the celebration. Although your congregation may wish to observe Children's Sabbath Day exclusively through the worship service, you can use the resources and suggestions throughout this book to extend the scope of the celebration and its purpose.

Forming a Planning Committee

When you have given some thought to the theme and format, take the idea of a Children's Sabbath Day to your church staff or the appropriate board or committee of your congregation for approval.

Once you have the agreement of the necessary committees and the approval of your board of council, your planning begins in earnest. Recruit a committee to help plan and carry out the day. Invite children and young people to join you. If you are trying to raise the awareness of the congregation about a particular issue, invite someone with information about and experience with that issue to work with you.

Convening the Planning Committee

Take time at the first meeting of the committee to get to know one another and to be clear about your task. Select a meditation from pages 11-20 to use in beginning your work together. Adapt it as necessary.

Present any preliminary decisions that have been made regarding the theme, focus, format, and scope for the Children's Sabbath Day. If the scope is still flexible, the next step is to determine the format of the celebration. The three most likely segments are the service of worship, the church school hour, and the fellowship time. You might choose to plan for one of these segments or for all three. You might choose to have a congregational meal or picnic as a part of the day. You may concentrate all your efforts on a single day, or use the Children's Sabbath Day as either the kickoff or the culmination of an education series on a theme related to children.

After you have selected the focus and format and determined the basic range of activities, recruit other volunteers to assist. Be sure to allow plenty of time to publicize this special day.

Promotion

Enthusiastic promotion is vital to build support, participation, and enthusiasm for the Children's Sabbath Day. Alert those in responsible positions — the choir director or church school teachers, for example — to any changes in the usual schedule well in advance.

Introduce the upcoming Children's Sabbath Day to the congregation through announcements in your church newsletter and worship bulletin. Plan to place the bulletin insert, found on pages 107 and 111, in your church bulletin one week in advance of the actual day. Prepare a press release for the religious affairs section of the local newspaper. Display posters, perhaps created as a church school activity, throughout the church to publicize the event. Reminders from the pulpit a few Sundays prior to the day are helpful as well.

Suggestions for the Service of Worship

- Use the bulletin insert, found on pages 37 and 38, in your Sunday church bulletin.
- Select scriptures that focus on children. See pages 21-23.
- Name specific needs of children during the liturgy. Include prayers for the needs and suffering of children, specifically naming needs that will be familiar to the congregation and praying for ministries with which the congregation is involved.
- In the prayer of confession, acknowledge our lack of compassion for or complacency about the suffering of children. Allow a few moments for the worshipers to meditate in silence on our failure to protect and sustain all of God's children.
- Include a special offering to meet the needs of children or to support a program serving children. The offering could be money, food, or letters to be sent to legislators. A mission project chosen by the children could be the recipient of the offering.
- During the worship service, project slides of the children of your congregation on a blank wall as statistics about children in need are read. This can be part of a sermon or the call to confession.

- Affirm the work and accomplishments of the children and teachers in the church school. Recognize the time, energy, and faithfulness of the teaching staff. During the worship service you can recognize the importance of their work as part of a Commissioning Service (see page 34).
- Decorate the sanctuary with banners or posters made by the children.
- The children and young people could enter the church in the processional at the beginning of the worship service carrying the banners they have made.
- The children and young people could read prayers and scripture lessons.
- The children could lead hymns or responsive readings.
- The children could greet worshipers as they arrive in or leave the sanctuary.
- A group of older children and young people might present a short drama for the sermon.

At the end of this section you will find three sample services of worship for a Children's Sabbath. Use them to get started and adapt them with the suggestions above and your own ideas.

Suggestions for Church School Groups

These suggestions can be used in church school groups or during a special time of celebration following a service of worship, such as at a congregational meal or picnic.

For all ages

- Select a mission project that provides services to children, such as a program for homeless children, a child care program, or a maternal and child health clinic. Contact the staff and find out how you can help promote or participate in its work. Plan an introduction to the project for the congregation with photographs or slides, or an on-site tour. Following this introduction, develop activities based on the suggestions from the staff to promote or support the program. Some of the introduction can be done in church school groups prior to the Children's Sabbath.
- Hold a poster party or essay contest on the focus of your Children's Sabbath. Include age categories from young children through adults. Display the winning entries throughout your church building or in the community. The prizes could be donations to a children's program of the winners' choice.
- Ask each church school group, including adults, to prepare a specific part of the service of worship for the Children's Sabbath. Provide them with options from this book. One person from the planning committee should be responsible for checking with each group and coordinating the service of worship.

Young children (ages three to five)

- Have the children decorate posters that are pre-printed with the slogan, "Please remember children in all that you do." Crayons, markers, or pictures cut from magazines can be used. Send the posters to elected officials in local, state, and national offices. Include a cover letter explaining the Children's Sabbath.
- Take a photograph of the children with their posters before you mail them. Display the photograph where your congregation will see it. If possible, have prints made for the children.
- Concentrate on helping the children see themselves as part of the congregation. They can help in the publicity for the Children's Sabbath Day by drawing pictures for fliers or the worship bulletin cover.

Older children (grades one through six)

- Make posters as suggested in the activity for young children.
- Talk with the children about the things for which they are thankful, including families, friends, pets, toys, and favorite foods.
- Help them write prayers of thanks for what they have. Display them for the congregation to see. Print them in the church newsletter or worship bulletin from time to time. Credit the authors.
- Make mobiles of their prayers of thanks. Have the children write them on cardboard shapes. Hang them with yarn or string from dowels. Balance a shape on each end of the dowel.
- Help them write a litany of thanks. The line for the response of the worshipers can be: "For this, we give you thanks, Great God." See the litany on pages 24-26 for a sample format.
- Have the children write new words to a familiar hymn tune. Use the focus for the Children's Sabbath as the topic for the new hymn stanzas. Sing this hymn as part of the service of worship for Children's Sabbath.

Young people (grades seven through 12)

- Use the meditations from pages 11-20 to begin church school or fellowship group meetings. Include time to discuss the meditation, using the questions provided or questions of your own. Focus on how young people can participate in speaking out for themselves and all children.
- Have them create a large banner for the Children's Sabbath you are planning.
- With the young people, create a list of ways they can act on behalf of children in your congregation, community, state, or nation. The list could include writing to legislators, volunteering at a children's shelter or day care center, tutoring, and working in a food pantry or emergency shelter. Check with programs in your area for some specific suggestions to offer the young people.
- After the list is created, or at the next meeting, provide ways for the group to volunteer, either together or individually.
- Discuss the teen pregnancy posters and ad campaign developed by the Children's Defense Fund. Ask: Why is this a problem for young people today? What do you think can be done to educate young people and to prevent teenage pregnancy?

Adults

- Develop a short-term study course on the needs and rights of children, to begin or conclude on the Children's Sabbath (see Section III).
- Organize an adult forum, In Celebration of Children, and ask a representative from each of the standing committees to highlight their committee's concern for and involvement with children.
- Invite persons from the congregation or the community to be on a panel to discuss the unmet needs of children and families in your community, state, or around the nation. Highlight effective programs. Provide a list of ways the group can support these programs.
- Secure copies of resolutions or statements passed by your congregation, regional body, or denomination regarding the rights and needs of children. Study them and talk to the appropriate committees or boards of your congregation about their implementation. (Refer to Section V for ordering information.)

An All-Church Dinner and Program

Many of the previous suggestions can be incorporated into a program following a meal together. The planning committee will want to answer these questions:

- Will you have everyone participate in the same activities, or will the activities be age-segregated?
- Will the meal be a potluck, or will a group prepare it?
- Will there be a presentation for everyone, to begin the program, or will people go to their choice of workshops at the beginning of the program and gather together at the conclusion?
- How can children and young people be involved in the planning and leadership?

Building On the Children's Sabbath Day

After you have held your Children's Sabbath, build on this opportunity to further your congregation's involvement with children and young people. If you celebrated the gifts and talents of children within your congregation, continue to include them in your worship services. If a local program for children was highlighted, keep its needs and progress before the congregation.

If you have made the congregation more aware of the needs and rights of children, continue to keep them informed and encourage their support and participation in speaking out for children locally, nationally, and internationally. Distribute information about pending federal and state legislation affecting children. Urge members to write letters expressing their opinions to the appropriate legislators.

A Sample Children's Sabbath, #1

Theme: God calls each of us, young or old, to action and service on behalf of others, especially of children.

Order of Worship

Prelude: Children's bell choir or youth duet on piano and flute.

Call to Worship:

Reader 1: From the quiet retirement of Abraham's and Sarah's old age,
when we feel too weary, too old, too weak,
God calls us.

Reader 2: From Peter's fishing net and Levi's tax concerns,
when we feel too busy with jobs or school or routines,
God calls us.

Reader 3: From the disciples' arms holding back the children, when we feel that we are the wrong age, gender, race, or social status,
God calls us.

All: **And so we assemble here now to heed God's call, and seek God's empowering Spirit.**

Hymn: *Colors of Day,* by Sue McLelland, John Pac, and Keith Ryecroft, or
Let There Be Love Shared Among Us, by Dave Bilbrough.

Prayer of Confession: (first through Litany, then in silence)

Leader: Each day in our nation, when 100,000 children are homeless, living on the street or in shelters,

All: **God, we confess that we avert our eyes, and pass by on the other side.**

Leader: Each day, when the air is filled with the cries of more than 800 babies born at low or very low birthweight,

All: **God, we confess that we cover our ears, and pass by on the other side.**

Leader: Each day, when more than 1,800 neglected or abused children yearn to be hugged,

All: **God, we confess that we withhold our touch, and pass by on the other side.**

Leader: Each day, when 27 children die from poverty, and 40 die or are wounded by guns,

All: **God, we confess that we harden our hearts, and pass by on the other side.**
God, open our eyes, ring in our ears, throw wide our arms, and soften our hearts, that we may receive these children in Christ's name, and so receive you who sent Christ. Amen.

Assurance of Pardon:
Christ came that we might know ourselves to be God's children. And so we are! Children of God, believe the Good News: through Jesus Christ, we are forgiven.

Old Testament Lesson: I Samuel 3:1-19
(Read in parts by: young person [Samuel], older person [Eli], narrator, and voice of God.)

New Testament Lesson: Luke 10:25-37
("Modern day" enactment of the Good Samaritan story by a youth group or intergenerational group.)

Develop a Brief Reflection or Sermon on Theme:
God calls all of us, young and old, to use our unique gifts and skills in service of others, especially of children in need. What can each of us offer?

Anthem: *Here I Am,* by Dan Schutte.

Offering:
Collect monetary offering as usual, perhaps designating it for a particular children's group or program. In addition, invite each congregation member to write, on a slip of paper inserted in the bulletin, a skill, action, talent, or amount of time they can give to help meet the needs of children. For young children (who could draw, rather than write), this

might mean helping a new child in class. These "offerings" could be deposited in a basket placed up front or in the regular collection plate.

Offertory Anthem: *Ubi Caritas*, from the Taize community (*Where Love and Caring Are, There is God*).

Prayer:
O God of infinite love and unending challenge, help us to listen to your call. Inspire us to use the varied gifts with which we have been blessed in the service of others, especially of children in need.

Keep us ever mindful, we pray, that when we provide adequate nutrition for the children who are hungry, we will have fed Christ.

When we welcome the "strangers" who are children without safe and loving homes, we will have welcomed Christ.

When we donate warm, well-made clothing for the children who are ill-clad, we will have clothed Christ.

When we have immunized all children against preventable disease and ensured adequate health care for all, we will have visited Christ.

When we care for juveniles in custody or the children of people in prison, then, too, we will have come to see Christ.

Help us to meet your challenge and reflect your love, so that one day it might be said that when we did this to the least of them, truly we did it to you. Amen.

Hymn:
Make Me a Channel of Your Peace, music by Sebastian Temple, or *Let Us Talents and Tongues Employ*, by Fred Kaan.

Benediction:
Let us go out to love our neighbors, especially children in need, and in so doing love God with all our heart, all our soul, all our strength, and all our mind. Amen.

Written by Shannon P. Daley
Religious Affairs Division
Children's Defense Fund
Washington, DC

A Sample Children's Sabbath, #2

A Service of Recognition

All: We are God's people, bound together in a faith community. Our church community begins with our knowing God as the source of all life. This same God, with steadfast love, calls us into a covenant relationship.

Leader: Our faith community is made up of many parts — people of all ages and from many places. Today you are each invited to covenant with each other to celebrate our teaching and ministry.

Leader (To the Teaching Staff): You have responded to a call to be active in this community of faith by volunteering to teach. Through this decision you acknowledge your interest in continuing to keep the promise given to our children at their baptism to nurture and care for them in the Christian faith. Are you willing to share your gifts and talents as you help them to grow in their understanding of God, Jesus, the Holy Spirit, and the church?

Teaching Staff: We are.

Leader (To Other Church School Support Staff): You likewise have agreed to help as a substitute, nursery care person, or juice mother. Are you also prepared to care and nurture our children as God has called us to do in love?

Church Support Staff: We are.

Leader (To the Parents): The purpose of our church school is to provide a program shared by both the church and the home. Do you promise to show an active interest in your children's church experience, and to reaffirm their baptism by mutually sharing and growing together in the Christian faith?

Parents: We do.

Leader (To the Church Staff): As a part of the church's faith community, do you as members of the church staff promise to reach out and be a resource, a support person, and help the church school staff grow in their understanding of our Christian faith?

Church staff: We do.

Leader (To the Congregation): You each, individually and collectively, are called to share in the nurturing and caring of our children. Having heard the promises of the church school teachers and staff, the parents, and the church staff, do you promise to support all of them?

All: We do.
We are all learners in our faith community — children, youths, and adults. Let us celebrate our joy of being faithful to one another in our covenant relationship.

A Local Congregation in Connecticut

From the Department of Christian Education and Youth
Connecticut Conference
United Church of Christ

HEALTHY BABY WEEKEND WORSHIP MODEL, #3

A sampling of worship resources developed for Healthy Baby Weekend 1990 by Indianapolis-area clergy and lay people (see pages 128-129, Model Health Program, for additional information). The Covenant on Infant Mortality and Suggestions for Citizen Action (found on page128) were included in this packet of materials for use by congregations celebrating Healthy Baby Weekend.

Options for Scriptural Texts and Themes

II Samuel 12. Nathan confronts David with his sin. David's child dies for the father's misdeeds. The story interprets the death as a sign of the covenant violated. What does our city's constantly high infant mortality rate say about the quality of our covenant? What other injustices are connected with our high infant mortality rate? What must we do to restore the covenant?

Genesis 15. God and Abram enter into covenant. Abram is to be our blessing for all the earth. All our children are gifts, signs of the eternal covenant, signs of blessing.

Call To Worship

The Good News is this:
- Pain and suffering have limits.
- We are not lost.
- The poor are loved.
- Resurrection is real.

Our world has other news. Bad news.
- Babies die.
- Parents grieve.
- Poverty grows.
- People blame others.
- Violence occurs.

Between the Good News and the bad news is the presence of God's people. We are called to let light illumine darkness, to elevate joy over gloom, and for truth to dispel evil. Come, let us be God's people today. Amen.

Litany

Leader:	Christ has brought good news to the poor.
All:	**Let us be partners in spreading this message.**
Leader:	Christ has proclaimed liberty to the captives.
All:	**Christ has set us free.**
Leader:	Christ promises sight to the blind.
All:	**Open our eyes that we might see.**
Leader:	Christ uplifts the downtrodden.
All:	**Let us look up, then, to proclaim the year of the Lord.**

Written by the Rev. Duane Grady
Northview Church of the Brethren
Indianapolis, IN

Litany

Leader:	We give you thanks, O God, for your life-giving power!
All:	**Thank you, God!**
Leader:	We give you thanks, O God, for those parents who nurtured us in the womb of their love!
All:	**Thank you, God!**
Leader:	We give you thanks, O God, for doctors, nurses, midwives, and those who lovingly brought us forth into the world!
All:	**Thank you, God!**
Leader:	We give you thanks, O God, for the many loving family members and neighbors who surrounded us with their loving touch and words as we first encountered our new earthly environment!
All:	**Thank you, God!**
Leader:	We lift up our prayers, O God, that every child of yours will be able to fully experience your joyful gift of life.
All:	**Hear our prayers, O God!**
Leader:	We lift up our prayers for those parents who struggle daily to care for their child, and for their own well-being.
All:	**Hear our prayers, O God!**
Leader:	We lift up our prayers for the medical professional community, that they will be able to use the gifts that you have given them so that they may sustain every newborn's life to maturity.
All:	**Hear our prayers, O God!**
Leader:	We lift up our prayers for ourselves, O God, and we ask that you sustain us and remind us of our calling to care for every person, young or old, so that we may all enjoy the fullness of life that you have given us and experience the fullness of your blessing.
All:	**Hear our prayers, O God! Amen!**

Written by the Rev. Phil Tom
Westminster Presbyterian Church
Indianapolis, IN

Dedication to New Life

In the tradition of the Disciples of Christ, a service of Dedication to New Life is performed for children and their families shortly after a new baby comes. Such a service could be planned for all children in the congregation on this day. Or a similar service could be held for all the unnamed children, that they might no longer be at risk. Here is a litany that could be used for such a dedication ceremony.

Leader: Having recognized the increasingly complex, nearly overwhelming problem of infant mortality in our city, this day has been designated Healthy Baby Sunday.

All: **As members of the human family, as believers in a God who affirms life, and as participants in the life of this city, we rise to the challenge of making this city a healthier place for babies and their families.**

Leader: The problem of infant mortality is not a problem with individuals. It is not a problem of the poor. It is not a minority issue. It is society's problem.

All: **We understand that, if we are to do our best to make the world a place where babies are healthier, we must first recognize and learn the widespread causes of infant mortality.**

Leader: While study is important, it means nothing if it is not accompanied by advocacy and action on behalf of those who have no voice.

All: **We confess that advocacy and action often scare us, but we are willing to risk status and reputation if that is what it takes to make the world a safer place for babies and their families.**

Leader: There is a resource available to all persons of faith that feeds and sustains all that we do.

All: **We are busy people, but not too busy to pray for babies who are conceived and born at risk, to pray for the families that care for those children, to pray for the church that is called to offer the sustaining grace of God to all who are in need, and to pray for ourselves, that our response might be pleasing in the eyes of God.**

Leader: Today is Healthy Baby Sunday in Indianapolis.

All: **Those of us who are woven into this community commit ourselves this day to each thread that makes us who we are — a beautiful, colorful, vibrant tapestry that reveals nothing less than the majesty of God.**

Written by the Rev. Rick Powell
Centenary Christian Church
Indianapolis, IN

Prayer

O God, Creator and Sustainer of all life, we come to you in prayer knowing that our individual prayers are heard, believing that our corporate prayers have power.

God, be with us this day. Comfort us as a mother comforts her child. Protect us from harm. Nourish us with word and with bread. Open our hearts. Guide our steps. We remember that prayer is a time to be encouraged and renewed as we seek the directing voice of our God.

Hear us now, O God, and lead us in the ways of justice so that as we pray for your protection and strength we might also seek this good news for others. We know that there are many for whom comfort seems a distant and abstract thing. God, you have created life and you bid us to protect and develop it.

In our midst and in our world, we hear the cries of those who suffer and of those who have not enough. Teach us to respond as you would have us, with compassion, with grace, and with hands that heed your vision of Shalom.

God, we recognize you as the author of life, hating nothing which you have made. Teach us to see your love in those for whom life is not a joy. We pray for the innocent, the lonely and pained. We pray for justice with all of its implications for those who suffer and for those who can change this suffering.

God, hear our prayers. Amen.

Written by the Rev. Duane Grady
Northview Church of the Brethren
Indianapolis, IN

BULLETIN INSERT *(see next page)*

How To Use This Bulletin Insert
- Cut out the bulletin insert and make enough copies for Sunday worship or your event.
- If appropriate, list a contact person in the space provided to assist those who want to get involved or learn more.
- Use the bulletin insert as a tool to announce an upcoming Children's Sabbath or study into action program on children.
- Include an explanation of the purpose of the insert in the bulletin and during announcements.
- Be creative! Design your own bulletin insert and make copies for Sunday worship and special programs and events.

WELCOME THE CHILD

Then [Jesus] took a little child and put it among them; and taking it in his arms, he said to them, "Whoever welcomes one such child in my name welcomes me, and whoever welcomes me welcomes not me but the one who sent me."

Mark 9:36-37

WHO IS ONE SUCH CHILD IN OUR NATION THAT WE ARE CALLED TO WELCOME?

One of the 2,400 children born into poverty each day...

One of the 100,000 children who are homeless each night...

One of the 719 babies born at very low birthweight each day...

One of the 1,629 children in adult jails each day...

One of the 1,849 children who are abused or neglected each day...

One of the 2,400 children who drop out each school day...

One of the 3,288 children who run away from home each day...

One of the 27 children who die because of poverty each day...

CHILDREN'S DEFENSE FUND

WHAT DOES THE LORD REQUIRE OF US?

To do justice...

- Call the mayor's and governor's offices to learn the rate of child poverty, homelessness, school dropout, teen pregnancy, and child abuse or neglect in our community or state. Ask what government measures or programs are addressing these problems. Express support for funding and expanding programs that work.
- Call or write our members of Congress to learn what steps they have taken or what legislative measures they support to address the needs of children, particularly those at risk or born into poverty. Urge them to make children one of our nation's highest priorities.

...and to love kindness,

- Visit a local program or organization that meets children's needs (such as an after-school tutoring program, shelter for homeless families, or a health clinic offering prenatal care classes for pregnant teens and low-income mothers), and ask how you can help.
- Support worship, education, and service opportunities to celebrate children, lift up their needs, and lead our congregation into deeper involvement in meeting those needs.

...and to walk humbly with our God. *(Micah 6:8)*

- Read Psalm 131:1-3, Proverbs 31:8-9, and Matthew 18:1-7. Reflect on what we, as God's people, are called to do to remove the "stumbling blocks" before America's children.
- Pray for the children who are not faceless statistics, but who are known and cherished by God, and whom we are called to welcome in Christ's name.

To learn more about what our congregation is doing to meet the needs of children, and how you might become involved, contact:

_____

Or contact: Children's Defense Fund
122 C Street, N.W.
Washington, D.C. 20001
Telephone (202) 628-8787

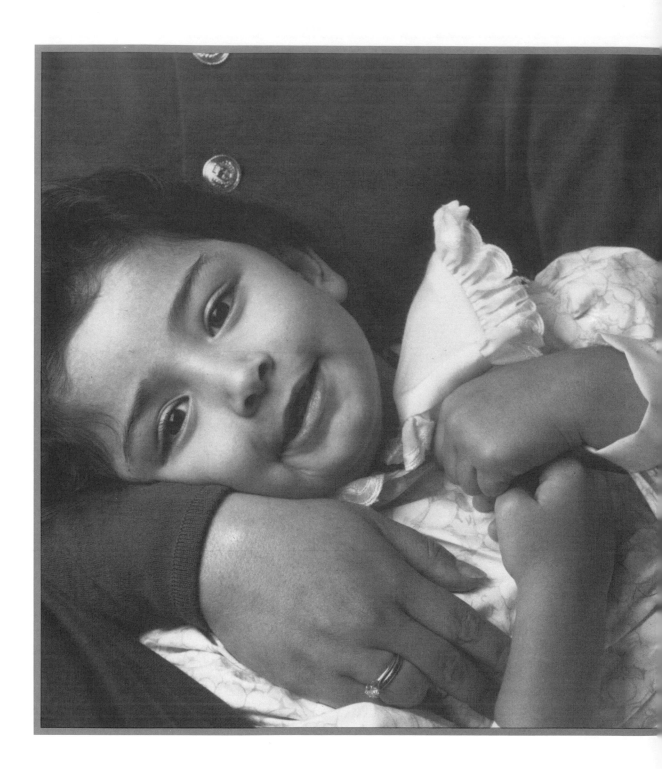

MAKING A DIFFERENCE FOR CHILDREN: STEP BY STEP

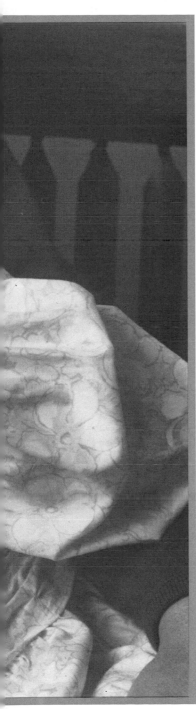

PHOTO BY NITA WINTER

A GUIDE FOR INVOLVING YOUR CONGREGATION

The opportunities for helping and empowering children are endless. However, no single congregation can do everything; nor is it appropriate for it to try. The key to effective action is to gain congregational support and determine a realistic plan of action. In this section you will find suggestions to help you discover:

- The interest and support for child advocacy in your congregation;
- The resources available in your congregation to meet the needs of children;
- The needs of children that are not being met adequately or at all in your congregation or community;
- How to match your congregation's resources to the existing needs; and
- Ways other persons and congregations have been advocates for children and their families.

For each of these initial planning steps a basic process is described and suggestions are presented that can help you. Because each congregation and community is unique, you may find other ways to streamline this process. Use some of these suggestions or develop your own process. What's most important is using the resources in your congregation to help meet the needs of children in a concrete, effective way.

Each congregation has its own personality and style of work. Some of that style is determined by the polity of the congregation and denomination. Some of it is determined by the professional leadership of the congregation. As you begin, be clear about the channels that you must use to gain approval and official sanction. Know the system for your congregation and work through it.

There is one word of advice that is important, however, no matter what your congregational profile or work style: Don't do it alone! Find an interested committee already at work or a few people in your congregation to work with you. Talk with your pastor or a staff person concerned about children and families. Child advocates work together. Find them in your congregation and go over this section together. Use it to help the children in your midst.

TAKING THE FIRST STEP — ASSESSING THE INTEREST

The following questions can help a committee assess the level of interest and concern for children in the total life of your congregation — in worship, education, and mission. You may want to ask additional questions, or the answer to one question may prompt another. The questionnaire is intended as a starting point, a place for you to begin to consider the range of activities that suggests how your congregation acts as a corporate child advocate.

The questions begin with issues that are closely identified with the life of every congregation and broaden until the concern is about social change throughout the nation. As you answer the questions, watch for the ones that are more difficult to answer and keep them in mind as you move ahead, because they indicate a stretching point for your congregation.

YOUR CONGREGATION, CHILDREN, AND FAMILIES

- How are the needs of children and families included in prayers for worship?
- How frequently are concerns of children and families mentioned in sermons? Are illustrations about children used primarily as amusement?
- What displays, such as banners or photo exhibits, reflect the talents of the children in your congregation? When was the last time they were displayed publicly?
- How does your congregation provide appropriate educational programs and other activities for children and youths?
- In the past three years has your congregation conducted a service of worship, such as a Children's Sabbath, that celebrates the special contributions and needs of children?
- How are children and youths encouraged to participate in the life of the congregation? Is their role primarily as observers? Are they usually age-segregated?
- What regularly scheduled activities are designed to help children build a spirit of giving and cooperation?
- Has your congregation, or a group representing it, offered a program to heighten awareness about children at risk in the past three years and offered ways to minister to such children?

- In the past three years has any course in the adult education program focused on children's issues and the Christian mission?
- What books or other materials does your congregational library or resource table offer on children's issues and child advocacy?
- Have the Christian education and social ministry committees ever worked together on a program or ministry affecting children in the congregation, community, or nation? If suggested, might they?
- Does your congregation, or a group within it, provide volunteers or financial support to a program serving children in your community? The nation? The world?
- Does your congregation conduct or house a child care program or other service for children, youths, and families?
- Does any committee or other group of your congregation work at political advocacy for children and families as an expression of your Christian mission?
- Does your congregation participate in political advocacy activities on domestic and international issues, for example by studying issues, writing letters, or joining groups such as IMPACT or Bread for the World?
- What methods, programs, and events have been most successful in motivating and empowering members of your congregation to act on behalf of others?

After your committee has talked together about your congregation's profile on children and families, identify the key persons and committees that have jurisdiction over and interest in your major concerns. If they're not already a part of your committee, meet with the clergy and professional staff of your congregation. Find out what concerns they see within the congregation and the community. They can provide you with a wealth of information about the congregation's ministry and a list of interested members in your congregation.

Your next task in this first step will be to raise the awareness of the congregation in general and to present a call to mission to individual members. There are several avenues for this. Some possibilities are listed here:

- Ask the worship committee or clergy to hold a service of worship that focuses on children and their needs. (See Organizing A Children's Sabbath Day, pages 29-38.)
- Ask boards and committees to use the meditations and discussions from this book.
- Offer to present programs for the various fellowship groups in your congregation. Provide them with the meditations and discussion suggestions on pages 11-20.
- Provide inserts for your church newsletter and worship bulletins from this book, such as the statistics or other noncopyrighted materials.
- Use **Section III: Developing a Study Into Action Program** to educate your congregation about and engage your congregation in one or several of the issue areas concerning children.

- Ask to speak about the needs of children during the time for church announcements in the worship service. Describe one area of the needs of children that you have discovered through your initial research.

Raising this awareness can help you gain initial support for whatever you decide to do later. However, it is an opening step that should never end. Your congregation changes throughout time. People come and go. Their interests and concerns also change. The single adult who listened with only mild interest last year suddenly will be all ears when married and pondering parenthood. The adult whose children are on their own may listen with concern but little motivation until she or he is a grandparent. Keep the needs of children and families in your congregation and community alive by providing information and stories regularly.

Finally, you need to decide how you will proceed. You may not want to make this decision firmly until you have determined your congregation's resources (see Step Two), but now is the time to consider it. You already have talked with the key persons and committees in your congregation. You may be ready to decide how you organize to move toward action. Four possibilities are:

- To work through an existing committee, such as the social concerns committee or the children's ministries committee. The latter may be the appropriate step if you want to include children and youths more fully in the life of your congregation.
- To combine two committees for a broader look at this issue, such as the local missions committee and the Christian education committee. Two such committees would work together to provide educational programs and opportunities that will lead to action within your community.
- To organize a task force made up of representatives of standing committees of the congregation and one or two persons from the congregation at large. This is often a good way to proceed when you hope to develop a new program or ministry.
- To organize an ad hoc committee (as small as two or three persons) to proceed until another plan for organization is needed. This is usually an interim group that will keep things going as more information is sought or support developed.

TAKING THE SECOND STEP — DETERMINING YOUR CONGREGATION'S RESOURCES AND THE NEEDS OF CHILDREN IN YOUR CONGREGATION AND COMMUNITY

I n Step One you may have discovered changes you already can make within the life of your congregation that will help children grow in wisdom and faith. You probably have begun to identify some needs of children that go beyond your congregation. Now it's time to move ahead by identifying interested members of the congregation and determining the amount of existing or potential support for programs to help children and families within your congregation and community.

ASSESSING YOUR CONGREGATION'S RESOURCES

Find out about the resources available within your congregation. Much of the information may be readily available from clergy and staff.

To gather the information, invite representatives of various age groups and committees to help you complete the resources information charts on pages 48-50. Ask your clergy and other staff members for suggestions as you put this group together. If staff members are not a part of your committee, asking them will provide an important connection between you.

Design your own chart, listing the individuals' names and indicating their particular area of interest. If you develop a questionnaire to include in a Sunday bulletin or your church newsletter, keep in mind that people generally prefer to check off items you've listed rather than to write in their

---

THE CONGREGATION: A VITAL ROLE

- The congregation is a community already committed to love of God and neighbor.
- Members know each other and work on projects together.
- There is a willingness to listen to the individual's ideas.
- Congregations can bring together a variety of skills and talents — manual trades, business experience, public service, expertise in communications — that are essential in running any project.

---

own answers.

Make sure that you include on your list those persons who have professional expertise, such as social work, medicine, nonprofit organization management, politics, or journalism, or those who have worked on a particular issue in the past. Don't overlook grandparents, parents, church school teachers, social ministry committee members, volunteers in community programs for children, and anyone else who has expressed a concern for children. Keep this list handy. Put it on a computer, if possible. Update the list regularly, adding new names and additional information. Refer to the list when you need committee members, particular expertise, or information and volunteers.

A COMMUNITY NEEDS ASSESSMENT: CHILDREN'S NEEDS AND THOSE WHO HELP MEET THEM

- How many children need child care? Is child care available?
- How many teenagers drop out of school?
- What proportion of our children grow up in poverty?
- How many incidents of child abuse are reported each year? Are the cases increasing or decreasing?
- Are teenage drug and alcohol abuse, gangs, or crime a problem in our community?
- What is the infant mortality rate in our city or state?
- How many teenagers become parents each year?
- Does our community have work opportunities for teens?
- How many of our children and families go without adequate public or private health insurance?

You probably don't have to look very hard to find children and families in your community or city who are struggling to survive. But how do you go about finding information on the type and extent of the problems that exist for children in your area and the agencies, organizations, and programs that currently serve children and their families?

Fortunately, you don't need to start from scratch or undertake a time-consuming research project. Your first step should be to talk with staff and members of your congregation who have an interest in children's concerns. Keep in mind that you are looking for organizations and individuals to help you determine the most critical needs of children and teens in your community and ways your congregation can complement existing community programs and efforts. A few well-placed phone calls can simplify the gathering of information and can build your connections within the community.

If you or members of your congregation would like to explore further what's happening to children in your community, and the organizations and resources that exist to meet children's needs, here are some suggestions to get you started:

- **What city, county, and state agencies can provide statistics and information on public programs and services for children and families?**
  Contact departments of health, welfare, social services, and youth services; police and law enforcement; state vital statistics bureaus.

- **What local organizations deal with the problems of children and families?**
  Look in your telephone book or local newspapers for child advocacy organizations and coalitions, child care resource and referral groups, child care licensing agencies, community youth programs, child service organizations, the March of Dimes, and others.

- **What roles do the public schools and teachers play in meeting and identifying the needs of children and families?**
  Check with the departments of education at local colleges and universities, your school board, and PTA.

- **What local organizations and agencies deal with children as part of a broader mission?**
  This list is just a beginning for you: ecumenical council or ministerium, religious charities, United Way, hospitals, Association of Junior Leagues, YMCA, YWCA, Church Women United, League of Women Voters, and American Association of University Women.

- **Who are the key people in your community with whom you want to establish and maintain contact?**
  Consider elected officials and those running for office, school board members, reporters who cover children's issues locally, and retired persons who have been active in children's issues.

Looking at the needs you have identified and the congregation's resources you believe to be available, which need matches the majority of your resources? Is it a pressing need? Do you have enough resources and potential support to work on this need? Can you begin searching for others with whom you can join forces?

For example, did you identify:

- Teen parents who need support and parenting skills? Congregation members with counseling or social work experience? Then consider organizing a parents' group, with child care when it meets. Or work in partnership with an organization that provides counseling and parenting training.
- Latchkey children who need after-school care? An unused room in the church, and adults or older teens with tutoring or camp counseling experience? Start an after-school program in the church. Borrow or buy a VCR and show movies; plan recreation activities; plan a quiet space for homework.
- Children failing in school? A youth fellowship group or singles' group eager for a weekly service activity? Set up an after-school tutoring program.
- Foster children who need permanent, loving families? Families in the congregation that would be interested

in foster care or adoption if given emotional and material support from the church? Set a goal for your congregation to see that one adoptable child in foster care is placed with an interested family, and plan a congregational material and emotional support system. Hold a series of meetings on foster care to encourage families in your congregation to care for foster children.

- Families needing safe and affordable child care? Available financial resources in your congregation? Build a financial partnership with a child care program serving low-income families and their children. Or set up a scholarship fund for families that need child care.

- Preteenagers and teenagers who need support and guidance? Members in your congregation who like to volunteer? Involve members in Big Brothers and Big Sisters organizations in your area.

- A high infant mortality rate in your city or state? A congregation with a strong emphasis on education? Organize an adult forum on maternal and child health issues. Invite local speakers and end with a plan of action.

- A high child poverty rate in your area? Congregational interest in changing public policies? Organize a letter-writing campaign to local, state, or national elected leaders on the need for more public investments in children and families.

A Congregational Resources Assessment

Human Resources

Name	Address/Phone	Interest/Expertise	Availability

(use additional paper if needed)

Financial Resources

• Monies budgeted currently for Mission and Outreach:

$_____

      Amount of that money that supports programs for children and families:

      $_____

• Monies budgeted for children and youth programs in your congregation:

$_____

• Special offerings or appeals to the congregation for programs related to children and youths:

$_____

• Your estimate of untapped financial resources in your congregation for children and youths:

$_____

Physical Resources

What, in each category below, is available for programming for children and youths? What existing resources could be made available if a program warranted it?

• Church building: _____

• Outdoor space: _____

• Audio-visual equipment: _____

• Toys and other play equipment: _____

• Office equipment (such as computers and photocopiers): _____

• Vehicles: _____

CHILDREN'S DEFENSE FUND

PUTTING IT ALL TOGETHER: MATCHING YOUR CONGREGATION'S RESOURCES WITH CHILDREN'S NEEDS

Level of Congregation's Interest and Expertise

	High	Low	Comments
Education:			
Community Outreach:			
Public Policy Advocacy:			

Available Resources

Financial _____   Property _____

_____   _____

_____   _____

_____

Equipment: _____   _____

_____   _____

People, Skills, Time
(Continue on additional paper)

_____ _____ _____

_____ _____ _____

_____ _____ _____

_____ _____ _____

_____ _____ _____

Most Critical Problems Facing _____

Children and Their Families _____

(Local and National) _____

_____

_____

Congregations, Organizations, and Programs Making
A Difference for Children

Name   Address   Phone Number

_____

_____

_____

_____

_____

_____

Resource Persons in the Congregation and Community

_____ _____ _____

_____ _____ _____

_____ _____ _____

_____ _____ _____

_____ _____ _____

_____ _____ _____

Other Items of Interest: _____

_____

_____

_____

PUTTING IT ALL TOGETHER:
MATCHING YOUR CONGREGATION'S
RESOURCES WITH CHILDREN'S NEEDS

(Sample)

Level of Congregation's Interest and Expertise

	High	Low	Comments
Education:		✔	mostly elderly members supportive but unlikely to participate
Community Outreach:	✔		
Public Policy Advocacy:		✔	a few key people with strong interest and experience, but no generalized interest in the congregation.

Available Resources

Financial *$4,800 from other churches & indiv. contributions $2,000 seed grant from indiv.*

Equipment: *VCR, piano, books, games, sports equip.*

Property *available M-F large fellowship hall with stage, kitchen, classrooms, gymnasium, small playground Park across street*

People, Skills, Time
(Continue on additional paper)

Bill and Mary Smith	*lunchtime supervisors*	*every day*
Jane Outer (high school senior)	*new games specialist*	*every day*
John Brown (university student)	*organize trips*	*once a week or as nec.*
Cindy Jones	*gym activities*	*every day*
Eatha Beadle *	*3rd grade teacher*	*M, W, F*
* member of area congregation / partner church		

Most Critical Problems Facing
Children and Their Families
(Local and National)

Inadequate schools/need for better education, drugs, esp. crack, neighborhood violence, need for safe place & supervision after school & during summer while parents work

Congregations, Organizations, and Programs Making
A Difference for Children

Name	Address	Phone Number
NJ govt. free lunch program		
Head Start (housed at Bethany Church)		
Urban Cabinet – coalition of local churches		
Greenwood Methodist Church		

Resource Persons in the Congregation and Community

Congregational Ministries Committee of Presbytery
Halo Farms -- willing to donate juice & food

Other Items of Interest: _Princeton Theological Seminary will pay for 2 seminary students to work with a summer program._

CHAPTER 3

SITE VISITS AND TOURS

One means of raising your congregation's or committee's awareness, motivating them, and helping select a specific program to support as a congregation is planning a site visit and tour.

A newspaper may quote statistics about infant mortality, but words on a page can be erased mentally. Seeing a three-pound infant connected by tubes to life-support systems leaves a much more profound impression. Personal experiences can set hearts on fire.

If you plan to invite members of the boards and committees of your congregation to visit a program, also invite community leaders and policy makers to join you. Such visits can stimulate your guests' sense of urgency about children's needs and a willingness to become involved and involve others.

SUGGESTIONS TO MAKE THE MOST OF SITE VISITS AND TOURS

- **List all the potential sites and visits related to the area of concern you have chosen.** If you have chosen health care, show both the problem, such as babies in neonatal intensive care units, and attempts to prevent the problem, such as a prenatal care program for low-income women. If your guests become too depressed, they will be unable to act at all.
- **After you have chosen the sites you wish to visit, determine whether you have any connection with these sites through members of your congregation.** If so, ask them to help you make the contact or to assist you in planning the trip.
- **Call each program.** Explain to its director the plan for your visit. Ask if you can come, and how large of a group the site can accommodate.
- **Visit the site and talk with the director before the tour is planned.** Be clear about your purpose and the type of information that you want the participants to gain. For example, if you are visiting a soup kitchen, is your concern about how it handles food donations, or is it the number of children fed each day? Work with the director so that the greatest impact can be made in a short amount of time. Encourage the director to tell an anecdotal story to illustrate the need for and impact of the program.
- **Ask for written materials from each site.** Provide the participants with some basic information ahead of time. Suggest that they read it and note questions they have.
- **Coordinate the logistics of the visit carefully.** If possible, travel in one vehicle. Be sure the driver is clear about where you are going and how to get there. Provide name tags for the participants.
- **Work with the directors of the programs to make the trip as valuable as possible for them and for you.** Directors are very busy people, often running understaffed and underfunded programs. Be considerate of the time you are taking.
- **Prepare the participants for the visits before you begin.** Site visits and tours are learning experiences, not spectator sports. It is difficult for a group touring a program not to appear to be "looking at the poor people receiving services." Ask the participants to be as unobtrusive as possible. Discuss the need to be sensitive to the privacy of the clients at the programs you visit. Should they recognize someone, it is better that they make no move unless the other person speaks. Needless to say, the identity of the clients should not be discussed after the visit.
- **The visit is not over when you walk out the door.** Plan to use the time between sites to talk about what you saw and how you felt. At the conclusion of the visits, plan time to talk over the experience and to discuss possible next steps. Consider these questions: How can we work in partnership with one or more of the programs we visited? How can we use the knowledge we have gained through these visits to help children and families? What actions are needed to support these programs — writing letters to legislators or newspapers, supporting services, or volunteering, for example?

BUILDING PARTNERSHIPS TO HELP CHILDREN AND FAMILIES

*A*s you have researched programs in your community and as you have read and heard about how other congregations have ministered to and with children at risk, you probably have realized that there is much to be done. In your probing perhaps you have found programs that are doing good things. There is no need to reinvent the wheel and come up with another program to serve the same children when you could help an existing program serve more children or improve what it already is doing. Perhaps you have identified a serious need, but you cannot find the resources in your congregation to provide a program. Don't give up; look for partners from other congregations or community groups to work with you. Pooling resources for the good of the whole community is good stewardship. Build on one another's strengths. Perhaps an after-school program is sorely needed and you have a group of retired teachers willing to work in it, but your church building is not located conveniently to the school. Ask congregations nearer the school to plan the program with you.

Begin a partnership small, but dream big. Working together for the first time takes some getting used to and ad-justing to one another's styles. Partnerships demand equality. Be clear about the resources, both material and human, that each partner will provide. Put decisions in writing so they can be communicated to others.

As you look for partners, consider institutions and groups that are not church-related as well. Another congregation may be your first thought, but consider nonprofit agencies that serve children and youths, ecumenical or religious social service agencies, ecumenical bodies, and child advocacy coalitions and organizations.

There are also various forms of partnerships. Some partnerships are formed to provide a financial base for a program. Others provide a pool of human resources, both volunteer and professional. Partners may offer in-kind services or contributions to meet an agreed upon level of support. If you are open to the possibilities, you can come up with other ways to forge partnerships to help children and families.

Communication is an important element in working with other groups. Plan from the beginning ways that the membership of each group will be informed and encouraged to support the program. Report to each group regularly. Encourage their questions and interest.

ONE EXAMPLE: A CHURCH WITH A SMALL MEMBERSHIP, STAFF, AND RESOURCES

Like many urban churches, Bethany Presbyterian Church in Trenton, New Jersey, has a small congregation of perhaps 90 active, worshipping members in a large church building that once housed a congregation of 1,500 and numerous activities and programs.

Bethany has a long tradition of ministering to area children by providing space for a Head Start program. As the new sole pastor, Reverend Patricia Daley, and others realized, however, the needs of the children extend beyond Head Start. In particular, many of the children who had begun attending Bethany's church school, like a large number of other children in Trenton, have additional pressing needs for safe, supervised enrichment activities during the summer while their parents work.

In assessing Bethany's interest and expertise, it became clear that the most widespread and sustainable support would be for concrete, visible neighborhood outreach programs. A review of the available resources revealed that Bethany's greatest assets are plenty of available space and equipment, a committed pastor, and an energetic core of volunteers.

As a small congregation, Bethany's financial resources are modest. However, a $2,000 seed grant, donated by an individual, made the dream of an outreach program for neighborhood children seem realizable, if it could be supplemented by creative identification of other resources. Bethany teamed up with Westminster Presbyterian Church, as well as other area and suburban churches with considerable financial resources.

In addition to the resources and support found in partnership with other churches, Bethany identified the federal breakfast/lunch scheme as a program already helping children, and was able to utilize it to supply free lunches. Princeton Theological Seminary offered to provide another valuable resource — a seminary student to work with the program all summer.

Bethany has found one of its greatest resources, however, in the neighborhood teenagers. By using 13- to 15-year-olds as junior counselors, Bethany simultaneously provides these older children with constructive activity and leadership skills development while filling its need for additional staff. Different churches in the Presbytery are invited to sponsor a junior counselor and pay her or his modest stipend. This, again, provides dual benefits, by supporting the teenagers while encouraging the involvement of a broader range of churches.

The success of Bethany's outreach program can be found in its creative approach to assessing needs and resources of the congregation and community, developing ongoing partnerships with area churches, and building on the strengths of the children themselves.

For more information, contact Reverend Patricia Daley, Bethany Presbyterian Church, 400 Hamilton Avenue, Trenton, NJ 08609, (609) 393-6318.

ANOTHER EXAMPLE: A CHURCH WITH A LARGE MEMBERSHIP, STAFF, AND RESOURCES

All Souls Church in New York City is a Unitarian Universalist congregation of more than 1,000 members. Its membership has considerable professional and volunteer expertise in children's issues. In the fall of 1987 a Children's Taskforce was formed to respond to the growing crises affecting children in New York City and the United States generally.

In its first year, the programming of the task force consisted of a Foster Care and Adoption Project, an Education and Advocacy Committee, a Welfare Hotel Project, a Tutoring Project, and a Boarder Babies Project. In the years since, these projects have been evaluated and changed to better serve the needs of the children as well as help the volunteers who serve them.

Because All Souls is a large congregation, it can afford to invest finances and personnel in a wide variety of children's projects. Still, the leadership of the Children's Taskforce knew the importance of matching the projects to the resources they had. They used essentially the same process advocated here, working at a small number of specific projects and using their volunteers and resources wisely. Their first goals were simple and the time frames for projects short. Their expectations were realistic. By keeping their minds and hearts open to adapting and adjusting programs as they developed, they were able to create successful programs that met the needs they had recognized. Though their profile may look overwhelming to you, their process and plan of work is within your reach.

For more information, contact the Children's Taskforce, The Unitarian Church of All Souls, 1157 Lexington Avenue, New York, NY 10021, (212) 535-5530.

DEVELOPING A STUDY INTO ACTION PROGRAM

PHOTO BY SUSIE FITZHUGH

How To Use
This Section

This section provides both a framework and resource materials for developing a Study Into Action program for your congregation. A Study Into Action program is a congregational series designed to engage participants in:

- Exploring the theological basis for involvement in social issues affecting children;
- Learning about specific issues as they affect children locally, statewide, and nationally; and
- Developing corporate or individual action plans to help make a difference in the lives of children.

You may choose one issue, such as child care, on which to focus a four-week Study Into Action program, or you may decide to study a number of different issues in succession. Whichever format you opt for, the framework and resource materials provided in this section will help you:

- Stimulate theological reflection on a particular issue or issues affecting children;
- Raise questions to consider throughout the course of study;
- Identify human resources in your congregation and community (as well as written and visual materials) to inform your Study Into Action group about the particular issue or issues; and
- Plan action steps for further education, community involvement, or public policy advocacy.

Chapter 1 sets out a format (and Leader Suggestions) for developing a Study Into Action program in your congregation. This program may be designed for an adult education forum, a youth group series, or an intergenerational program.

Chapters 2 through 7 contain materials on each of the six major issue areas (child care and Head Start, vulnerable children and families, education, homelessness and housing, maternal and child health, and youth self-sufficiency and teen pregnancy prevention). For each issue you will find the following resources: scriptural and secular quotes; sample reflection questions; a brief introduction to the current problems, goals, policies, and programs related to the issue area; a worksheet to help you identify sources of information in your community; and examples of action steps.

CHAPTER 1:

A FOUR-PART FORMAT FOR A STUDY INTO ACTION PROGRAM

WEEK 1: THE FACES OF _____ (THE ISSUE, FOR EXAMPLE, HOMELESSNESS)

Begin the session by presenting one of the suggested scriptural or secular passages. Raise the questions that will encourage members to reflect on the faith basis for addressing the issue.

If the introductory text was distributed prior to the first session, allow time for initial questions or discussion. If it was not, distribute the text now and either summarize the key issues or allow time for the group to read through it.

Invite someone with personal, hands-on experience working with those affected by the issue to speak. Contact a social or community service organization, or perhaps an area church with a program related to your issue. Ask the speaker to describe, with anecdotes, the real impact of the issue on children. Invite the speaker to show slides or share photographs. A short video may also help to personalize the issue.

If possible, arrange for a site visit (see page 53) of a facility or program dealing with the issue. If the visit will take place directly after the education hour or worship service, arrange for extended child care of group members' children. Alert group members in advance of the scheduled site visit.

WEEK 2: _____ (THE ISSUE) IN OUR COMMUNITY

Begin with prayer, or perhaps spend the beginning of this session collectively writing a litany based on what group members saw and felt and learned in the first week on the site visit.

Invite a speaker from a local agency who can educate your group about the scope of the problem in your community and particular programs currently available. Ask the speaker if there are materials you can photocopy and distribute ahead of time or at the conclusion of this session.

Alternatively, you may want to incorporate the worksheet provided for each issue area in Chapters 2 through 7 as part of your Study Into Action course. At the end of the first week, distribute the sheet and have group members select which agency, program, person, or aspect of the problem they will research between the first and second session. Make the second session one in which each member shares what she or he has learned.

Plan an activity or action for the end of this session, or for during the week. For instance, the group may want to write letters to the mayor telling her or him of its interest in the issue and requesting further information. A sample letter may help people write their own letters. Alternatively, some group members may want to write letters to the editor of your local paper.

WEEK 3: THE LARGER PICTURE OF _____ (THE ISSUE)

Begin with prayer, or with another brief time of reflection and discussion on a scriptural passage.

Invite speakers from, or informed about, state- and federal-level agencies to discuss the national scope of the problem and state and federal policies and programs.

Learn ways that people can effect legislative change on the state and national level. For this session's action, the group may decide to make phone calls to the offices of its members of Congress to ask that children's needs be at the top of the agenda. If the group learned about a particular piece of legislation, it may want to focus on that. Or the group may wish to write to members of Congress about a particular bill or legislative agenda. (See Section IV for ideas and reproducible materials.)

At the end of this session the group should decide whether it will pursue collective action on behalf of children, or whether each member individually will seek out a form of advocacy based on her or his interests and schedule.

WEEK 4: FROM STUDY INTO ACTION

Invite a trio composed of an educator, an outreach person, and a public policy advocate to present alternatives for action.

In the resource materials for each particular issue you will find specific examples of how education, outreach, or public policy advocacy action might be tailored to a particular issue. Photocopy the pages and distribute them to group members to stimulate brainstorming.

If the group has decided on collective action, use this time to determine whether it will focus on education, outreach, or public policy advocacy, and make concrete plans to follow through. You may want to invite key church leaders, staff, or committee members to attend this session to help plan what the group will do as it moves from study into action. Refer to **Section II: Step by Step** and **Section IV: Giving Voice to the Voiceless** to help you plan.

If the group has decided not to pursue action collectively, but instead individually to engage in some form of child advocacy, use the Pledge of Commitment form for this last session. Make a photocopy for each member. Have each group member decide which form of action — education, outreach, or public policy advocacy — she or he will pursue, and fill in the appropriate line of the pledge. Have the entire group sign the back of the pledge, to affirm the corporate spirit and support of the group as each member pursues an individually chosen form of action. The important final component of the pledge to be filled out indicates which organization or individual a group member will work with. This moves the pledge beyond a statement of good intentions to a starting point of action.

Then set a date in the next month or two to get together for a potluck dinner or a group breakfast before church to share what action each of you has undertaken on behalf of children.

Plan time for reflection and sharing about this Study Into Action program, and for evaluation. You may wish to develop a simple Act of Dedication as the group moves from study together into action.

Leader Suggestions for Developing a Study Into Action Program

Stimulate Theological Reflection on the Particular Issue Affecting Children

Using the scriptural and secular passages at the beginning of the resources for an issue area (or from Section I of this book), you may want to spend the first 15 or 20 minutes of each session in prayerful consideration and discussion of our God-given mandate to protect children, focusing particularly on the issue at hand.

Raise questions that will help your group reflect on the scriptural passages, and that will guide your study of the issue area. These questions will forge the link for the participants between the more customary Christian education-style study and the less familiar study of a social issue. Good questions prepared by the leader will help the group see the connection.

For instance, if the Study Into Action program is about youth development and teenage pregnancy prevention, have the group read Psalm 144:12: "May our sons in their youth be like plants full grown, our daughters like corner pillars, cut for the building of a palace."

After the group members have read the passage, ask them to reflect upon and discuss the following questions:

- What kind of environment, or what supports, do the sons and daughters of our nation need to flourish "like plants full grown" and to be as solid and stable as "corner pillars of a palace"?
- What kind of education, job preparation, and information on issues related to sexuality and family life do they need?

Identify Education and Information Resources for Your Study Into Action Program

The descriptions of issue areas in the following chapters are intended as general introductions, and may be reproduced. If possible, distribute photocopies to group members before the first session, so they will have time to read the introductory material before the first session.

However, you will need to identify sources of more detailed, in-depth information that will be useful for studying an issue as it relates to your community. *You don't have to be an expert yourself* to plan this Study Into Action program. You just need to identify, invite, and involve knowledgeable people in your congregation and community.

The resource materials for each issue area include a worksheet-style page to facilitate this process. As the program *leader*, you can use the worksheet to help you plan and prepare this Study Into Action program, before it begins. Alternatively, you may want to distribute the worksheet to *group members* during the actual program, so that they can participate in identifying information resources and researching the issue.

Either way, when you have identified an organization or individual you may decide to invite them to address the group as a speaker, to request written material on the issue or their organization, or to obtain information over the phone. Section II, page 46, also suggests sources of information and key people to contact regarding community problems, programs, and policies.

Plan for Your Group To Decide Into What Action This Study Will Lead

You can incorporate small, immediate actions into your program while laying the groundwork for a more substantial and sustained course of action. Making a site visit after church (see page 53) the first Sunday, telephoning your state legislator's office the next week to learn about his or her voting record on children's issues, and writing to your members of Congress on the third Sunday are all immediate actions the leader can plan and incorporate into the group program. Think through the actions in advance to determine what group members will need (addresses and phone numbers, sample letters, pens, and stationery, for example).

Another desired outcome of the program of study is *continued* action on behalf of children. Some groups may choose to initiate a sustained *corporate* action as they conclude the program of study. For other groups, however, moving from study into action may mean that each member, with the newly gained knowledge of the problem and programs in the community, decides upon an action which she or he will pursue *independently*. Either way, some possibilities for the group to consider are:

- **Further education.** This may be of yourselves, the broader congregation, the community, or public leaders.
- **Outreach involvement in the community.** This may be through existing programs in your own church, community organizations, or partnering with other churches, or it may mean establishing a new program.
- **Advocacy in the public policy arena.** This action may take different forms, and may be directed at public policy on the local, state, or federal level.

PLEDGE OF COMMITMENT

Now there are varieties of gifts, but the same Spirit; and there are varieties of services, but the same Lord, and there are varieties of activities, but it is the same God who activates all of them in everyone. To each is given the manifestation of the Spirit for the common good.

I Corinthians 12:4-7

To one is given through the Spirit the utterance of wisdom, and to another the utterance of knowledge according to the same Spirit....

I Corinthians 12:8

I pledge myself to help educate others about the needs of children and how we can minister to those needs. Specifically, I pledge to:

_____

"Then the righteous will answer him, `Lord, when was it that we saw you hungry and gave you food, or thirsty and gave you something to drink? And when was it that we saw you a stranger and welcomed you, or naked and gave you clothing? And when was it that we saw you sick or in prison and visited you?'

"And the king will answer them, `Truly I tell you, just as you did it to one of the least of these who are members of my family, you did it to me.'"

Matthew 25:37-40

I pledge myself to undertake an outreach activity to minister to children's needs. Specifically, I pledge to:

_____

Speak out for those who cannot speak, for the rights of all the destitute. Speak out, judge righteously, defend the rights of the needy.

Proverbs 31:8-9

I pledge myself to advocate for public policies that benefit children. Specifically, I pledge to:

_____

The name, address, and telephone number of an organization or individual with whom I will work to fulfill my commitment to a ministry of child advocacy:

_____

_____

_____

As a community of faith, we are called to support each other in our ministries. The following people pledge to support me in my ministry to children in need, as I will support them in theirs:

[Jesus said,] "I will not leave you orphaned; I am coming to you. In a little while the world will no longer see me, but you will see me; because I live, you also will live. On that day you will know that I am in (God), and you in me, and I in you. They who have my commandments and keep them are those who love me; and those who love me will be loved by (God), and I will love them and reveal myself to them.

"I have said these things to you while I am still with you. But the Advocate, the Holy Spirit, whom (God) will send in my name, will teach you everything and remind you of all that I have said to you."

John 14:18-21, 25-26

_____
Signature   Date

CHAPTER 2:

CHILD CARE AND HEAD START

Look on my right hand and see —
there is no one who takes notice of me;
no refuge remains to me;
no one cares for me.

Psalm 142:4

As the major provider of child care in the United States, the church has a special responsibility to help raise ethical questions about child care. It is the obligation of the church to advocate a coherent, comprehensive, inclusive, and above all, equitable public policy regarding child care. As it approaches public advocacy for child care, the church must be guided by its concern for all sectors of society.

The National Council of Churches of Christ, Policy Statement on Child Day Care

For every child in Sunday school, eight children are in church-housed child care on Monday.

Called to Act: Stories of Child Care Advocacy in Our Churches, *The Child and Family Justice Office, National Council of Churches, 1986*

If the child is safe, everyone is safe.

G. Campbell Morgan, "The Children's Playground in the City of God," The Westminster Pulpit, *(circa 1908)*

"Whoever welcomes one such child in my name welcomes me, and whoever welcomes me welcomes not me but the one who sent me."

Mark 9:37

REFLECTION QUESTIONS

- Ordinarily we think of adults as the authors of the Psalms, and thus tend to identify as adults with their writings. Try reading Psalm 142 as though a child is speaking. How does this help you understand the need of a child for security and self-esteem? How is safe and affordable child care connected to self-esteem?
- Churches are the major providers of child day care in this nation, according to the statistics gathered by the National Council of Churches of Christ, USA. What theological and biblical basis can you give for the church involving itself in child day care? Consider the two scripture quotations above in regard to this question.
- Jesus admonishes his followers to receive children in his name. What does that mean to you? What requirements does it place on the church? On individual members of each congregation?
- Today, one of two mothers is in the work force. What support is needed for them and their children? How can your congregation "take notice" and provide "refuge" for children?

CHILD CARE

On a recent rainy day in Cincinnati, Ohio, Marquise Freeman woke at 5:30 a.m. to dress and feed her two children, one and two years old. At 6:30 she and the children boarded the first of two crosstown buses to her cousin's house. After leaving the children with her cousin, Marquise took another bus downtown to her office job. That evening she reversed the trek, arriving back home at about 8 p.m.

Marquise and her children are exhausted by this daily commute. She dreams of sending her children to a child care center near her apartment, but she can't afford it. She is in the midst of a divorce, receives no child support, and earns just $6.07 an hour. She has applied for child care assistance from the state, but there is a long waiting list. Meanwhile, Marquise and her children spend long hours each day riding buses to and from her cousin's house.

Hundreds of thousands of working parents like Marquise need safe, accessible care for their children but can't afford it. Many others, especially parents of infants, are having trouble finding good quality child care at any price.

The child care crisis reflects the radical changes that have occurred in America's family and work life in the past two decades. The number of mothers in the work force is increasing every year, and most of these mothers work because they must. One out of four of today's working mothers is the primary wage earner for her children. Many two-parent families now need two salaries in order to afford the basic necessities.

As a result, more than half of all mothers with preschool-age children now are employed, and that includes mothers of infants. More than half of all women with babies younger than one year are either employed or looking for work. Two-thirds of mothers with school-age children have jobs outside the home.

Most employed parents traditionally preferred having relatives care for their children, but that option has become far less available as more and more grandparents and other relatives are either in the work force themselves or live too far away. Today, working parents rely on a variety of child care arrangements, depending on what they can afford and what is available. An increasing number of parents are choosing center-based child care, particularly for older toddlers and preschoolers.

While communities and schools increasingly recognize the importance of offering before- and after-school care for school-age youngsters, an alarming number of children — more than 1.9 million between the ages of five and 13, according to the U.S. Census Bureau — take care of themselves after school. The true number of children left unsupervised may be much larger than the reported number, however, since many parents find it difficult to admit that they are leaving their children alone.

Even very young children sometimes are left unsupervised by working parents who fear they will lose their jobs if they stay home with their children when their child care arrangements fall through. A few years ago, Linda Grant of Dade County, Florida, found herself in such a predicament. She relied on friends and relatives to care for her two children, three-year-old Anthony and four-year-old Maurice, since her paycheck could not cover the cost of child care. Some days these arrangements fell through and Linda left the boys on their own. On one such day, Anthony and Maurice climbed into a clothes dryer. When they shut the door, they tumbled and burned to death.

The High Cost of Child Care

A nationwide survey of child care costs in 1989 reported that the average cost of full-time care for one child was $3,432. Parents with tight budgets often feel they must settle for the cheapest child care available, even though they may not be satisfied with the quality. A few years ago in a neighborhood near Chicago, 47 youngsters were discovered being cared for in a basement by only one adult. It's unlikely that any of the parents of those children were happy about the arrangement, but, at $25 a week, the program cost only one-third as much as most child care in the community.

Although many parents cannot stretch their paychecks far enough to meet their family's basic needs and pay for decent child care, only a small proportion of low-income parents are lucky enough to receive child care assistance. In almost every state the money available for subsidized child care is grossly inadequate.

Families' Needs Are Not Being Met

Even if every family could afford decent child care, their child care problems would not necessarily be over. In many communities there simply isn't enough good quality child care to meet the demand.

Among parents of young children who were polled nationally in 1989, two of five said there were not enough programs for preschoolers. And only one in four parents said there was a sufficient supply of child care for infants. Union Bay Child Care in Seattle, for example, recently had 18 infants and toddlers enrolled in its child care program, but it had a waiting list of 233.

More child care is available for preschool children than for infants, but many preschool programs operate only part-day. Young children often have to shuttle among as many as three caregivers in a single day, a stressful regimen that child development experts say is not good for young children.

The lack of reliable, affordable child care prevents many parents from going to work to support their families. In a 1986 study of welfare participants, nearly two-thirds of those who responded said that child care was their primary problem in seeking and keeping jobs. Seventy-six percent of the women surveyed who had given up job hunting cited child care difficulties as the reason.

Quality is Critical

Child care should be more than a parking place for children while their parents work. Children and society both benefit when child care assures children's safety and provides a solid foundation for healthy social development and school success. Child development experts say that young children should be cared for in small groups with a high ratio of staff to children, in order to assure close adult supervision and lots of adult-to-child interaction. Good child care includes activities geared to a child's age and skill level, proper health and safety practices, and lots of communication between caregivers and parents so that children's individual needs are met. Since young children need predictable routines and relationships in order to feel secure and develop the ability to trust, there should be little turnover among a child's caregivers. For their part, caregivers need at least some basic training to help them understand the special needs of young children, deal with parents effectively, and cope well with emergencies and stress.

Every child needs and deserves high-quality child care, but it is critical for children living in fragile families — for example, those headed by a single or very young parent, an abusive parent, or by one who abuses drugs or alcohol. The tragedy is that these are the children most likely to receive low-quality care. In effect, these children are placed in double jeopardy; since their home situations make them especially vulnerable, they are at greater risk of being negatively affected by chaotic, unstable, and nonnurturing child care than are other children.

The Response to the Child Care Crisis

To make sure that every child who needs it has good child care, our society must actively engage the child care crisis on many levels — public and private, local, state, and national. Such a far-reaching commitment requires new thinking about children and child care.

Traditionally, Americans have viewed children as a "private asset," for whom parents are solely responsible. As a result, many legislators as well as private citizens have considered state-funded child care as a kind of welfare that benefits certain working parents at the expense of the general public.

But, in fact, children are both a private asset and a public resource. Our whole society benefits when we nurture and develop our human resources as fully as possible. Since good child care contributes to our children's development, it is in our national interest to make it a public priority, not just a family concern.

Community organizations and employers have an important role to play in responding to families' needs for good child care. Historically, no community organization has responded more actively than churches. America's churches are the single largest provider of child care in the country, supplying about one-third of all center-based care. In addition, many nonprofit organizations sponsor child care programs, and local United Way chapters have both invested in child care and earmarked funds for child care scholarships for low-income children.

Government's Role

Although some states have taken small steps in recent years to address the problems of cost, quality, and supply of child care, the resources for such efforts generally have been very limited. The states have tended to use federal funds to help subsidize child care for low-income families. The money most states use for child care subsidies comes from a federal grant that the states also use to support many other child welfare and social service programs. In 1988, after being adjusted for inflation, the grant amounted to only 53 percent of its 1977 value. As a result, many states cut back the amount they spent on child care for poor families. Twenty-three states served fewer children in 1988 than they did in 1981, despite a larger need.

As it became increasingly apparent that states could not solve the child care problem without greater help from the federal government, child care advocates around the nation began working together to develop federal child care legislation. After four years of intense effort by parents, child care providers, and local and national child care advocates, Congress passed the nation's first comprehensive child care legislation in October 1990. The act established a new grant to the states to improve child care affordability, quality, and accessibility.

States must use three-quarters of the new grant money to help low-income families pay for child care and to increase availability and quality. Families that earn up to 75 percent of the state's median income are eligible for assistance. States must offer eligible parents vouchers to help pay for child care of their choice. The providers, which can be relatives, family day care providers, religious institutions, or private child care centers, must be licensed, comply with state and local law, and meet minimal requirements established by the child care law.

States are required to use the remainder of the grant to expand child care services for preschool and school-age "latchkey" children and to improve the quality of child care through such activities as improving caregiver salaries and training, strengthening quality and safety standards, and shoring up state monitoring and enforcement efforts.

In addition, federal money will be available for child care under the Aid to Families with Dependent Children (AFDC) program. This new money will fund child care for parents who would need to go on welfare without help in paying their child care bills.

The 1990 legislation represents a victory for working parents and their children — and for the nation's future, the quality of which depends on fully developing our human resources. The act is an important step toward developing a child care system that is of consistently high quality in every state. But it is just a first step. There is still much to be done before all American children have the kind of child care experiences that contribute to their full physical, emotional, and cognitive development.

HEAD START

In Head Start, the nation has a highly successful preschool program for disadvantaged three- to five-year-olds that ideally should be available to every eligible child. Since its beginning in 1965, Head Start has enabled hundreds of thousands of low-income children to start school healthy and well-prepared to learn. And, for many Head Start graduates, the program's positive influence remains evident long past elementary school.

Experts in early childhood development say that Head Start's success in preparing children for productive lives is based on two important elements. First, the program is comprehensive, meaning that it seeks to ensure each student's health and general well-being as well as his or her cognitive development. Recognizing that children who are undernourished or have untreated medical problems cannot learn efficiently, Head Start provides hot meals, immunization against childhood diseases, and screening and treatment for vision, hearing, and other medical and dental problems.

Second, Head Start supports children's healthy development by strengthening their families. Head Start teaches parents to see themselves as the primary teachers and advocates for their children. In addition, Head Start provides family counseling and referral to other community resources and government assistance programs.

Head Start trains parent volunteers to work in the program, encourages them to continue their own education, and draws much of its paid staff from among former Head Start volunteers. More than one-third of Head Start's paid staff members are parents of former or current Head Start students.

The combination of comprehensive services and family involvement pays off for Head Start children. Research consistently shows that children who attend Head Start score higher on achievement tests and are more likely to meet the basic requirements for school than control groups. Once in school, Head Start graduates are less likely to be placed in special education classes or to be held back in school than other children from similar backgrounds.

What's more, the general benefits of Head Start and similar preschool programs persist into young adulthood. Studies of young adults who participated in preschool programs similar to Head Start show that these young people are more likely than their peers to be literate, employed, or enrolled in postsecondary education. They are less likely to be school dropouts, teen parents, dependent on welfare, or in trouble with the law. Both the business community and Congress have estimated that every dollar the nation invests in high-quality preschool programs saves about $6 in the cost of special education, welfare, and crime later on.

Despite its record of success, Head Start never received enough funding to both increase enrollments and cover rising costs. During the 1980s the program attempted to comply with federal pressure to expand enrollments modestly by cutting back on staff training and program improvements and by deferring such expenses as salary increases for teachers and staff. By 1990 the amount Head Start spent per child was less in inflation-adjusted dollars than it was in 1977. Experts were beginning to warn that Head Start's quality would be compromised unless it received funding to improve salaries, increase staff training, and make other program improvements.

The landmark reauthorization of Head Start in 1990 reflected both its widely acknowledged cost-effectiveness in preparing children for school and the need to take specific action to assure its continued quality. The four-year bill creates the potential for yearly increases in Head Start enrollment (subject to appropriations by Congress) until the program is able to serve all eligible children starting in 1994, at a cost of $7.7 billion. At the time the program was reauthorized, Head Start was serving only about 25 percent of eligible children.

To ensure Head Start's continued effectiveness Congress earmarked more money for quality improvements, including funds for staff training, and established new criteria for classroom teachers. The reauthorization also approved a new transition program to continue Head Start's comprehensive services for children after they enter school and will allow funds to be used for full-day, full-year child care for Head Start students whose parents work.

What Can You Do To Meet the Urgent Needs for Child Care?

Educate Yourself and Others

- Write an article for your church newsletter summarizing what you have learned about the child care needs of families in your congregation and community. This is important information to present to people who have no need for child care and may be unaware of the stress finding it places on families.
- If your church already houses a child care program, discuss with the director how that child care ministry can become more visible to the congregation. Perhaps a small bulletin board could display class photographs, with a description of the program and periodic events or needs.
- Write an article for your local newspaper summarizing what you have learned about the child care needs in your community. Or talk with the staff of the newspaper and suggest that such an article or series be developed.
- With other congregations and child care organizations, sponsor a community-wide Child Care Day to focus attention on existing programs and services.

Get Involved in Your Community

- Enter into a partnership with a congregation providing child care for low-income families. Provide toys and equipment, financial support, or volunteer assistance.
- Organize a fund-raising activity to benefit a child care program, or set up a scholarship fund to help parents who cannot afford child care.
- Develop or house an after-school child care program or full-day child care program in your church building. Excellent resources to assist you are available from the Ecumenical Child Care Network (see page 132).

Advocate for Quality Child Care

- Write to your members of Congress about the child care needs in your community.
- Join a child care coalition in your community or state.
- Speak with groups of business leaders or individual executives, encouraging them to take an active role in providing and advocating for quality child care. Provide information for them about the advantages to them when workers need not worry about care for their children.

CHILD CARE AND HEAD START INFORMATION RESOURCES WORKSHEET

Child development expert: (try professors at a local community college or university) _____

_____

Speaker yes ☐ no ☐ Send materials yes ☐ no ☐
Ask about: what child care or preschool education should be; what environment, activities, nurturing, and discipline young children need for optimal development.

Comments/information: _____

_____

_____

_____

Local child care or Head Start program: _____

Speaker yes ☐ no ☐ Send materials yes ☐ no ☐ Site visit yes ☐ no ☐
Ask about: number served; number on waiting list; costs; needs; resources; regulatory requirements and provider's opinion and enforcement of them; barriers and limitations programs face; services to low-income, nonwhite, and special-needs children.

Comments/information:

_____

_____

_____

Church sponsor of child care or Head Start program: _____
Speaker yes ☐ no ☐ Send materials yes ☐ no ☐ Site visit yes ☐ no ☐
Ask about: process and costs to sponsor/partner a child care or Head Start program, as well as those questions listed above.

Comments/information: _____

_____

_____

_____

Community advocates for child care: (look in the telephone book under Child Care Information and Referral, or ask the three previous contacts) _____

Speaker yes ☐ no ☐   Send materials yes ☐ no ☐

Ask about: local issues, differences in providers in the community, view of the day care needs in the community, current legislative push or desired actions, membership, etc.

Comments/information: _____

_____

_____

_____

State Department of Social or Human Services: _____

Speaker yes ☐ no ☐   Send materials yes ☐ no ☐

Ask about: state policy on quality and regulatory issues, affordability issues and policies, relevant statistics, current legislative items, etc.

Comments/information: _____

_____

_____

_____

Child Care Action Campaign, 330 Seventh Ave., New York, NY 10001, (212) 239-0138.

Send materials yes ☐ no ☐

Ask about: information on child care, state child advocacy contacts.

Comments/information: _____

_____

_____

National Council of Churches Ecumenical Child Care Network, 475 Riverside Drive, Room 572, New York, NY 10115-0050, (212) 870-3342.

Speaker (from local affiliate) yes ☐ no ☐   Send materials yes ☐ no ☐

Ask about: membership, local affiliates/contacts, etc.

Comments/information: _____

_____

_____

_____

National Head Start Association, 1220 King Street, Suite 200, Alexandria, VA 22314, (703) 739-0875.

Send materials yes ☐ no ☐
Ask about: information on Head Start.

Comments/information: _____

_____

_____

_____

Children's Defense Fund, Child Care Division, 122 C Street, N.W., Washington, DC 20001, (202) 628-8787.

Send materials yes ☐ no ☐
Ask about: current agenda, legislative items, desired actions.

Comments/information: _____

_____

_____

_____

National Association for the Education of Young Children, 1834 Connecticut Avenue, N.W., Washington, DC 20009, (202) 232-8777.

Send materials yes ☐ no ☐
Ask about: information on child care, and state and local contacts who may be working on advocacy.

Comments/information: _____

_____

_____

_____

CHAPTER 3

EDUCATION

Train children in the right way,
and when old, they will not stray.
Proverbs 22:6

America invests a smaller portion of its gross domestic product in education than 13 other industrialized countries.
Economic Policy Institute

REFLECTION QUESTIONS

- Read *Greenless Child* and *Children Learn What They Live* on page 26. What do the biblical passages above and the contemporary poetry have in common? How do they relate to the education of children? At home? In the church? In the community?
- What kind of environment does each child require so as not to be a "greenless child"? What kind of environment should our schools provide to help all children achieve to their greatest potential? What prevents schools from fulfilling this goal? What part does the church have in assuring this environment for all children?
- Read aloud *Children Learn What They Live*. Who are the children in your community who live with criticism? With hostility? With ridicule? With shame? Tolerance? Encouragement? Praise? Fairness? Approval? Acceptance and friendship? What do these children have in common? How are they different?
- Read Matthew 18:1-7 on page 22. Think about what you do in one day's time — at home, at work, in recreation. How much do you depend upon your ability to read, write, and communicate effectively to hold your job, to parent, to care for others, to enjoy leisure time? How would an inadequate education be a stumbling block in your day-to-day activities? How would it be a stumbling block to reaching life goals?

EDUCATION

America's educational system is in trouble. Far too many American students are not learning what they will need to become productive workers and citizens in the twenty-first century. Consider these facts:

- Only half of American 17-year-olds who are in school can compute using decimals, fractions, and percents. Fewer than half can understand, summarize, and explain the kind of writing found in encyclopedias or high school textbooks; only 28 percent can write a persuasive argument.
- In international math and science tests given to students in the United Kingdom, Spain, Ireland, Korea, and three Canadian provinces, American 13-year-olds ranked near the bottom in science and last in their ability to solve math problems.
- American school children know less geography than school children in Iran, and less science than school children in Spain.

American employers are confronting these realities every day. The New York Telephone Company had to test some 60,000 applicants in 1987 to find 3,000 people to hire. When IBM Corporation installed millions of dollars worth of computers in its Vermont factories, the company had to teach employees high-school algebra before they could use the computers.

Our Nation's Future Depends on a Fully Educated Work Force

In the coming decades, the mismatch between the needs of American employers and the number of qualified workers will grow worse as a result of several trends. First, our economy is simultaneously exploding with jobs that require high-level skills and finding less and less need for unskilled workers. Second, the proportion of young workers in our country is shrinking. In the year 2000 we will have 14 percent fewer Americans between the ages of 18 and 24 than we did in the mid-1980s. And third, between now and the year 2000 nearly one-third of those who enter the work force will be from minority groups, which are disproportionately poor and undereducated.

If our nation is to maintain a high standard of living and compete effectively in the global economy, every American child — regardless of race or economic background — must receive a first-rate education. This means that schools must improve for all students, but especially for poor and minority children.

Students Who Need the Most Get the Least

In general, poor and minority students get the worst of everything our educational system has to offer. These students go to the most run-down schools, they are assigned the least-skilled teachers, and they use the oldest textbooks. They have the fewest number of computers available for classroom instruction, the most inadequate libraries, and the barest science labs — if they have labs at all.

Part of the explanation lies in the fact that some poor and minority students live in communities where the tax base is not large enough to support decent schools, and the states have not taken adequate steps to equalize school funding. In Texas, for example, the poorest school district has been spending $2,100 per student per year, while the wealthiest school district has spent about $19,000.

Recently, courts in Texas and Kentucky have ruled that such vast disparities in school financing are unconstitutional and have ordered the legislatures in both states to create equitable educational systems. But funding for schools should be equalized in every state; in addition, schools that historically have been shortchanged must be given extra resources to eliminate the deficiencies created by years of inadequate funding.

Many Americans balk at the idea of spending more on our schools, even to equalize opportunity for all students. Part of this reluctance comes from the misconception that the United States spends as much or more on education than other industrialized nations. In fact, the United States spends a *smaller* share of our gross domestic product on elementary and secondary education than most other developed countries. According to the Economic Policy Institute, when spending on education in grades K-12 is related to the size of the school-age population in each of 16 industrialized countries, the United States spends less than 14 of them. Only Australia and Ireland trail behind us.

Resource-poor schools are not the only obstacle to good education for disadvantaged students, however. Even when poor and minority students attend predominantly white, middle-class schools, they often are educationally neglected as a result of their disproportionate assignment to lower-track classes.

In theory, tracking students according to perceived ability should help teachers do a better job of teaching children with different abilities. But tracking is based on an outdated and inaccurate notion that intelligence is a single, unchanging capability, when in fact intelligence is a collection of diverse capabilities that may be developed or not, according to children's experiences.

Tracking defeats both democratic values and academic achievement, according to educational researcher Jeannie Oakes and teacher Martin Lipton in their book, *Making the Best of Schools*. Poor and minority children disproportionately are assigned to the lower tracks, then receive less of everything that is educationally desirable. Low expectations and watered-down courses for students in average and below-average tracks mean that the 62 percent of American children who are placed in those tracks receive a mediocre education at best. Students in high school vocational tracks don't even get better jobs as a result of their training.

Moreover, research does not support the idea that students in the top track learn more because of tracking. When they learn more — and often they do not — it's because they are assigned skilled teachers and their course of study is more demanding, explain Oakes and Lipton. Given the same high expectations, demanding curricula, and skilled teaching, students in the lower tracks also would become high achievers.

Schools that Help All Students Achieve

A number of schools around the country already are paving the way toward educational excellence for poor and minority students. Garfield High School in Los Angeles is now one of these schools, but when math teacher Jaime Escalante joined the Garfield faculty in 1974, the school was one of the worst in Los Angeles. According to Escalante's biographer, *Washington Post* journalist Jay Matthews (*Jaime Escalante: The Best Teacher in America*, New York: Henry Hall and Company, 1988), a thriving gang system "sparred with a disheartened group of teachers," producing "something that often resembled street theater more than education."

Outraged that the teachers expected so little of their students, Escalante set about making sure that *his* students, at least, actually learned mathematics. Down the hall, a math teacher whom Escalante referred to as "a Ph.D. in fractions without denominators" gave his students puzzles to play with while he read the newspaper.

Slowly, Escalante's fierce belief in the Garfield students' unawakened abilities began to rub off on other teachers. With support from a like-minded principal, Escalante began offering a class to prepare students for the College Board's Advanced Placement Test in calculus, an effort dramatized in the movie *Stand and Deliver*. Building on Escalante's example, a group of teachers systematically expanded the Advanced Placement course offerings, eliminated courses in the regular curriculum that lacked academic challenge, and began requiring more advanced-level coursework for all students.

As a result, between 1981 and 1989 the number of Advanced Placement Tests administered annually to Garfield students increased from 56 to 503. In 1986 Garfield students accounted for fully one-third of the national total of second-year Advanced Placement calculus tests administered to Latinos. And in 1988 Garfield produced more Latino calculus test-takers than did the entire state of Arizona.

The Characteristics of Effective Schools

According to Oakes and Lipton, effective schools differ in specifics, but they share many crucial characteristics. These educators suggest that parents and other concerned citizens look for the following characteristics in order to judge whether a school is providing a quality education for all of its students:

- The teachers and administrators believe that all of their students can succeed academically, and
- The children themselves believe they can succeed as a result of hard work and persistence.

Every classroom is a lively place, where:
- The curriculum is rich, complex, and related to students' real experience.
- Lessons require the students' active participation and promote their working together.
- Evaluation and grading are private, focus on the specific learning the child has or has not accomplished, de-emphasize comparison with other students, and encourage hard work.

In addition, effective schools:
- Establish clear goals and develop concrete action plans to achieve them;
- Insist that teachers and administrators accept individual and collective responsibility for their students' achievement;
- Evaluate teacher and staff performance and provide assistance or additional training in keeping with the schools goals; and

- Consistently involve parents in the school and in their children's education in significant and positive ways.

Educational Achievement Is a Shared Responsibility

Every sector of society has a vital role to play in making sure that our schools improve and that all children are educated for productive lives. Parents, of course, are the first educators. Ideally, they lay the groundwork for learning and reinforce the schools' efforts by creating a learning atmosphere in the home. Some parents aren't sure how to help their children, however. Churches and other community organizations can assist by organizing parents' groups, for example, that offer information about how schools operate and how parents can help children learn. These groups can also support parents' efforts to get more involved in their children's school and make the best of the education that is offered.

Churches also can supplement parents' efforts to boost their children's achievement. After-school tutoring programs, mentoring programs, and extracurricular activities can provide academic help to children who need it. These activities should be designed to build bridges between school work and the real world and to give children opportunities to discover their own special talents and enthusiasms. Disadvantaged children particularly need opportunities to develop the self-confidence and satisfaction that come from undertaking a significant project and seeing it through to a successful conclusion.

Churches can help educate communities about educational issues by providing opportunities for the public to hear about and discuss school reform in the context of our nation's economic needs and democratic values. For example, all concerned citizens need to learn more about teaching and learning strategies that improve schools for all students without relying on tracking to address student differences. To encourage lasting school reform, citizens must know how to evaluate schools both for quality and equity of education, how to hold schools accountable for the quality of education they provide, and how to be effective advocates for adequate and equitable school funding.

America's schools can be both democratic and educationally excellent, and responsible citizens must insist they be both. Our nation's future depends on it. For more information, order a copy of *An Advocate's Guide to Improving Education*, $4.50, from CDF Publications.

WHAT CAN YOU DO TO IMPROVE OUR PUBLIC EDUCATIONAL SYSTEM?

Educate Yourself and Others

- Attend school functions. Go to the open house or student events and productions. Meet the teachers and administrative staff.
- Sit in on school board meetings. Find out the issues first-hand.
- Study the school budget. Does each school in your area have adequate resources? How well is education funded?

Get Involved in Your Community

- Volunteer to tutor children who need extra help. Select a subject you like. Talk to teachers in your congregation to find out how to proceed. Perhaps you can tutor at school during the day, or in the evening in an existing tutoring program.
- Work with others to raise funds for special needs in the school. Hold a carnival or auction to provide equipment that is not in the school budget. You'll have fun and meet other parents, too.
- Walk the routes that children take to school. Are they safe? Do traffic signs alert drivers to the daily presence of children? Are there crossing guards at difficult corners? If not, talk with the principal of the school to find out how to correct the situation.
- Ask the children you know about their schooling experiences. What is fun? What is difficult? Become a listener for their concerns. Take an interest in their homework. Provide encouragement when the child is down. Your interest and encouragement will let the child know that you think education is very important.
- Set up a literacy lab. The illiteracy rate in our nation is appallingly high for a developed country. Work with schools to set up programs where adults can learn to read, learn English, and where children can get help in reading.
- Meet with representatives of the school board to put together an "adopt a school" program. Open up the possibility to congregations, businesses, and service organizations.

Advocate for the Improvement of Education for All Children

- Get involved in school board elections.
- With the help of other community groups concerned about education, plan a one-day conference for local and state educational leaders and decision makers to focus on particular educational issues, such as the high drop-out rate among minority students or the involvement of business and community groups in the educational process.
- Know how your school board members are chosen. If they are elected, vote in school board elections. If they are nominated, submit names of qualified persons. Then stay informed about the actions of the board. Let the board know of your satisfaction as well as your displeasure.

EDUCATION
INFORMATION RESOURCES WORKSHEET

Local tutoring program: _____

Speaker yes ☐ no ☐   Send materials yes ☐ no ☐   Site visit yes ☐ no ☐

Ask about: number served, number on waiting list, resources, description of students' needs. Who supports program? How was it established?

Comments/information: _____

_____

_____

_____

_____

Local Parent Teacher Association: _____

Speaker yes ☐ no ☐   Send materials yes ☐ no ☐

Ask about: what they see as the pressing problems, needs. What have the successes been? Innovative programs? Is there tracking? Are all parents involved?

Comments/information: _____

_____

_____

_____

School Board superintendent or member: _____

Speaker yes ☐ no ☐   Send materials yes ☐ no ☐

Ask about: current issues on agenda; funding — how it compares with other schools; how school's skills/achievement level compares statewide, nationwide; dropout rate; etc.

Comments/information: _____

_____

_____

_____

National Education Association state chapter: _____

Speaker yes ☐ no ☐   Send materials yes ☐ no ☐

Ask about: issues on their agenda, desired action from membership/nonmembers, etc.

Comments/information: _____

_____

_____

_____

American Federation of Teachers state chapter: _____

Speaker yes ☐ no ☐   Send materials yes ☐ no ☐

Ask about: same as above.

Comments/information: _____

_____

_____

_____

Children's Defense Fund, Education Division, 122 C Street, N.W., Washington, DC 20001, (202) 628-8787

Send materials yes ☐ no ☐

Ask about: current legislative items, desired actions.

Comments/information: _____

_____

Also consider contacting: local principals, teachers or students in your congregation, student council members; ask them what is working, what is needed, etc. Think about a site visit to an urban school; walk the halls, flip through the textbooks, look at the playground.

CHAPTER 4

VULNERABLE CHILDREN AND FAMIILIES

Father of orphans and protector of widows
is God in his holy habitation.
    God gives the desolate a home to live in,
he leads out the prisoners to prosperity,
but the rebellious live in a parched land.
    Psalm 68:5-6

Speak out for those who cannot speak, for the rights of
all the destitute.
    Proverbs 31:8

Every 26 seconds of each day, an American child runs
away from home.
    Every 47 seconds, an American child is abused or ne-
glected.
    Every seven minutes, an American child is arrested for a
drug offense.
    Children's Defense Fund analyses

A child's tears move the heavens themselves.
    Traditional saying

Imagine our surprise now to turn and see that despite
our great defenses our homes have been pillaged again. Our
children abused. Our wives battered. Our parents abandoned. Our homes infected with strange diseases: anorexia,
bulimia, alcoholism, drug abuse, the suicide of adolescents.
The bonds of our most solemn commitments are put to the
test in our homes.
    *James Carroll, "Our Homes, God's
    House," speech at St. John the Divine,
    New York, 1985*

"Whoever welcomes you welcomes me, and whoever
welcomes me welcomes the one who sent me. Whoever welcomes a prophet in the name of a prophet will receive a
prophet's reward; and whoever welcomes a righteous person in the name of a righteous person will receive the reward
of the righteous; and whoever gives even a cup of cold water
to one of these little ones in the name of a disciple — truly I tell
you, none of these will lose their reward."
    Matthew 10:40-42

REFLECTION QUESTIONS

- Throughout the Old Testament, the people of God are
  regularly admonished to care for orphans and widows,
  the powerless in the ancient society. The verses from
  Psalm 68 are one example of this message. Orphans are
  certainly among the powerless of our society. Who else
  are our "orphans" of today? How are children powerless in our society and culture?
- Consider together the biblical quotes above and the
  quote from James Carroll's speech. Note the title of his
  speech: "Our Homes, God's House." As parents, what
  is our calling and ministry to children and youths? As
  Christians? As equals with children and youths in the
  people of God?
- Although some commentaries suggest that "little ones"
  in the quote from Matthew refers to a group broader
  than children, the reference is clearly to the vulnerable
  ones in society and children are in that group. How do
  we give "even a cup of cold water" to children and
  youths? Especially to the most vulnerable children and
  youths in our community and world?
- Read the passage from Matthew several times. Instead
  of "little ones" substitute the names of groups of vulnerable children, such as infants born of drug-addicted
  mothers, children living in poverty, children who are
  homeless, youths who cannot read, and girls who are
  pregnant. What is the "cold water" that you can offer to
  each of these groups? This exercise can be used as a
  meditative exercise by substituting the names of vulnerable children you know for "little ones."

VULNERABLE CHILDREN AND FAMILIES

More and more we hear stories about a rapidly increasing population of vulnerable children and families and a severely overburdened child welfare system charged with meeting their needs. Here are just a few of the disturbing facts:

- An estimated 2.4 million children were reported abused or neglected in 1989, a 10 percent increase over the 1988 figures, and an increase of almost 150 percent since 1979.
- An average of three children a day died of some form of maltreatment in 1989. Homicides have replaced motor vehicle accidents as the number one cause of injury-related deaths among children younger than one in the United States.
- Estimates of the annual number of babies exposed to drugs before birth are now as high as 375,000.
- The Centers for Disease Control estimate that 10,000 to 20,000 children — disproportionately poor and minority children — will be infected with the AIDS virus in 1991. And projections of the incidence of AIDS among teens are being revised upward.
- Homeless families with children have become the fastest growing segment of the homeless population in many communities. An estimated 100,000 children are homeless each night.
- The proportion of American children who were poor in 1989 (19.6 percent) was higher than in any year between 1966 and 1980. And children who lived in families headed by parents younger than 25 had an astounding poverty rate of 44.7 percent.

Any one or two of these trends would create conditions for children that would strain the resources of our child welfare system. Together, these trends are overwhelming the system's capacity to respond. About 360,000 children now are living apart from their families in the care of the child welfare system — a 29 percent increase since 1986. If current trends continue, that number could reach half a million by the year 2000.

A System on Overload

Increasing reports of child abuse and neglect are forcing child welfare agencies to devote more and more resources to investigation and intake. As a result, preventive efforts to support and improve family functioning have not increased to meet the need. Nor has an adequate supply of foster family care been developed. Some children who enter care are simply dumped in emergency shelters where they don't have even basic protections, let alone good care.

It is particularly troubling that infants and very young children are entering state care at greater rates than ever be-

fore. In New York State the number of children age four or younger entering care for the first time more than doubled between 1984 and 1988, and in the Washington, D.C., metropolitan area there was a 40 percent increase in children younger than two entering the system between 1987 and 1989. Nationwide, 42 percent of the children entering foster care in 1988 were younger than six, compared with 37 percent in 1985. Many of these very young children were drug-exposed before birth, and many of the infants have no families to go home to.

The need for good foster homes becomes more urgent every day. But the sad reality in many states is that the supply is dwindling, partly because children entering care are increasingly troubled and have very special needs, partly because of increasing pressures on parents to work outside the home, and partly because reimbursement to foster families has fallen far behind the costs of adequately supporting a foster child. In some communities foster parents are paid less each week for caring for a child than a kennel operator receives for boarding a dog.

In early 1989 Florida had such a shortage of foster home beds that the state had to pitch tents to shelter abused, neglected, and abandoned children who had no other place to go. And in both Maryland and New Jersey agency staff had to put children in motels because they could not find enough foster homes.

The abandoned infants who linger in hospital wards as "boarder babies" are among the most heartbreaking evidence of the foster care system's inadequacy. These babies — some of whom have never been out of doors in their entire first year of life — are medically ready for discharge, but there are no foster families to care for them.

The child welfare system also suffers from a terrible shortage of trained, qualified child welfare workers to look out for vulnerable children. Low salaries, inadequate training and supports, and high rates of staff turnover and burnout weaken the system's effectiveness. Huge caseloads and crushing responsibilities make it impossible for child welfare workers adequately to support families where children are at risk, or to keep close check on children in out-of-home placements.

Needed: New Responses

There always will be a need for family foster care and residential treatment facilities for children who have very specialized treatment needs or whose families cannot be preserved. To make sure there are enough good foster homes and treatment facilities for the children who really need them, the experts argue, our child welfare system must not overuse out-of-home placement. These experts insist that a child should be separated from his or her family only *after* other interventions have been exhausted and only when it is clear the child cannot otherwise be protected. But a new emphasis on keeping families together must be accompanied by a new kind of help that protects children's safety at the same time it improves family functioning. This help may never turn vulnerable families into model families, say the experts, but it can enable many families to function adequately, nurture and protect their children, and remain intact.

One kind of special support for families — generally the most intensive — is called family preservation services. In a family preservation program, a child at imminent risk of being removed from the family is left in the home if the family agrees to participate and the child can be protected adequately. A trained professional or team of professionals with a small caseload of two to four families is available to the family on virtually a 24-hour-a-day basis for up to three months. The staff spends time with the family in the home, concentrates on active, practical aid in solving the family's immediate problems, gives on-the-spot instruction in and help with parenting, and assists the family in linking up with other family support systems in the community. The highly intensive but short-term intervention is aimed at involving the entire family, supporting the family's own goals, and building on the family's strengths in order to increase its ability to cope.

Many communities also are developing less crisis-oriented programs to strengthen families' abilities to care for their children before problems intensify. These "family support programs" generally are based on the assumptions that a child's development is related to the strength and health of the parent — child relationship; that most parents want and are able to help their children grow into healthy, capable adults; and that all families need help at some time, but not all families need the same kind or intensity of support.

Like family preservation, family support programs focus on families' strengths and help them supplement their own resources with community resources offered by employers, churches, and community organizations. Most programs rely on voluntary participation and try to reach families as early as possible. Often the programs are housed in accessible neighborhood drop-in centers, and often they include a home visiting component. Many programs offer comprehensive services, meaning they treat the family's needs as an interrelated whole and try to provide a wide range of assistance that may include parenting education and parent support groups, cooperative child care, assistance in obtaining health care and job training, special supports for young parents, and hotlines for child abuse prevention.

An Agenda for Change

Ideally, every community should have a range of adequately staffed and funded services for vulnerable families. The available services must begin with preventive programs to strengthen family functioning and improve families' abilities to nurture their children. For families in crisis, the continuum should provide intensive family preservation services that treat the whole family's needs and preserve the family unit whenever possible. There must be a variety of quality options for caring for children outside of their homes when that is necessary. And finally, for children in care who cannot be reunited with their families, there should be vigorous efforts to find permanent adoptive families.

Churches and other community organizations can play an important role in making sure their communities offer a variety of supports to vulnerable families. Churches can organize their own family support programs or "adopt" ongoing programs that need assistance. Churches also can enrich the experience of foster children through a variety of efforts and can help provide new permanent families and foster families for children by recruiting adoptive and foster parents.

At another level, churches also can become voices for change in the child welfare system. Churches can advocate for public policies and programs supporting preventive family services that reduce the need for unnecessary out-of-home placements. It also is important to advocate for policies and funding that will improve the system for children who must be removed from their homes.

WHAT CAN YOU DO TO IMPROVE SERVICES FOR VULNERABLE CHILDREN AND FAMILIES?

Educate Yourself and Others

- April is Child Abuse Prevention Month. Sponsor a special program to educate your congregation about child abuse and domestic violence and steps that can be taken to prevent it and to assist families where abuse has occurred. Consider dedicating a Sunday sermon each April to the theme of preventing child abuse and neglect.

- Thanksgiving week each year is National Foster Care and Adoption Week. Earlier in the month sponsor a special program to inform your congregation about the needs of foster children in your community and about the need for adoptive families and what they can do to help. Share with them calendars of local events being planned to celebrate Foster Care and Adoption Week so they can become more involved.

- Have your youth group prepare a directory of family resource and support programs in your community and learn how these programs can benefit from your congregation's support.

- Join with other religious congregations and community groups in sponsoring a one-day conference on successful programs in your community and state for serving high-risk children and families. Make a special effort to include programs that can benefit from volunteer contributions.

- Write to the national headquarters of your denomination and ask for information on programs for high-risk children and families that are operated by congregations in other communities.

Get Involved in Helping Children and Families in Your Community

Supporting families and preventing child abuse and neglect

- Sponsor parenting education programs for members of your congregation and others in your community. Conduct separate sessions for parents of young children, elementary school children, and teenagers. You may want to cosponsor these sessions with schools in the area served by your church.

- Have your congregation adopt a family in need of assistance and offer that family ongoing assistance and support. Assist the family with its basic needs, such as employment, food, and housing, but also arrange for children in your congregation to serve as peer companions for children in the family.

- Encourage senior citizens in your congregation to volunteer for the Foster Grandparent Program if there is a chapter in your community. If not, establish a program whereby you team senior citizens with teen parents in your congregation to offer them ongoing counsel and support. The senior citizens involved in the program may want to sponsor a Mother's Morning Out program one day a week, when parents can bring their children to the church for a couple of hours while the parents engage in specially organized activities.

- Adopt a social worker in your community's public department of children and family services and help support that worker by responding to the unmet needs of the children and families he or she is serving. The worker may ask for basic supplies, such as food, clothing, bedding, or health care supplies; for financial assistance to get the family through a crisis; or for help with home repairs, transportation, child care, or other services.

- Encourage members of your congregation to serve as respite care parents for children who are in foster care and whose foster parents need temporary relief from their full-time responsibilities. Although this might be done on an informal basis, there may be a special training program in your community for respite care providers, especially for those caring for children with special needs.

- A growing number of communities are establishing various systems staffed by volunteers to ensure that children in foster care get the attention they need in the court process and are reviewed periodically and not allowed to drift endlessly with no attention to reuniting them with their birth families or moving them toward adoption. If your community has a Court Appointed Special Advocate program or a Citizen Foster Care Review Board, urge members of your congregation to volunteer their services.

- Consider establishing a visiting center in the facilities of your church where birth parents can visit in comfortable surroundings with their children who are in foster care. Senior citizens could be available to assist local social workers with transportation for both the foster children and their birth parents. Senior citizens, together with teens from the youth group, also might provide on-site child care.

Finding adoptive families for children

- Encourage members of your congregation to consider adopting children with special needs, particularly children who have various mental, emotional, or physical disabilities, are older, are members of minority groups, or are part of a sibling group. Offer to cooperate with outreach activities being conducted by adoption agencies in your community. Incorporate a flier in the bulletin, sponsor an informational meeting, or let adoptive parents have a recruitment stand in the lobby after your service. Or you can participate in a One Church, One Child program operating in your community.

- Establish a Permanent Families Now fund for a local adoption agency that places children with special needs for adoption. These dollars could be used by the agency to waive fees for families approved to adopt special needs children, or to assist with other nonrecurring costs related to adoption that otherwise create barriers to permanence for these children.

- Adopt a crisis nursery in your community, and offer members of the staff the support they need. Such support may include material items, financial assistance, or help from volunteers. For example, senior citizens in your congregation may set up a transportation network to enable parents to visit their children on a regular basis. Or you may want to hold a baby shower several times a year to collect clothes and other items that the nursery supplies to parents in need.

Assisting children in foster care

- Designate four Sundays a year as Foster Care Sunday and ask members of your congregation to bring in certain supplies or make financial contributions to assist children in foster care in your community. Contact social workers at your local department of children and family services or the foster parent association in your community to determine the greatest needs at the time.

- Establish a tutoring and peer mentoring program for children who are in foster care in your community.

- Establish a scholarship fund to support participation by children who are in foster care in various extracurricular programs or summer activities in your community.

- Make arrangements with one of your denomination's colleges to provide a full tuition scholarship each year to a child in foster care from your community. Find a host family in your congregation, preferably a graduate of that school, who will offer the student ongoing emotional support throughout the school year.

- Many of the young people "aging out" of foster care at 18 or 19 have no family or friends to whom they can return. Get volunteers from your young adults group who are willing to serve as community sponsors for these young people. Your public agency may have a formal program of this sort, or your congregation may want to team up with a private agency that has children in its care.

- Encourage members of your congregation to consider becoming foster parents. Give foster parents who are in your church the opportunity to share their experiences with others. Set up a network of families who are available to offer assistance to the foster families when emergencies arise.

- Sponsor a post-adoption support group for families who have adopted children with special needs. Sponsorship might involve making space available for monthly meetings, offering clerical support for the group's regular communications, offering child care assistance for parents who are attending the meetings, or providing a portion of the salary of the group facilitator.

Support Policy Improvements for Vulnerable Children and Families

- Join with other child advocates in your state to push for greater investments of public funds in family support and family preservation services for vulnerable children and families. Set a goal of having at least one program in each county of the state. Start first with those counties where the majority of children in the state live. If your state already has several successful pilot programs, support an initiative to expand the programs statewide as part of a comprehensive system of services.

- Push your state officials to examine the growing numbers and costs of children in out-of-home care in your state. Urge them to look not only at increases in children in the care of the child welfare system, but at the juvenile justice and mental health systems as well, as children in the three systems often have very similar needs. They also should look at trends and make projections about future increases. Data of this sort can be very useful in making the case for greater investment in family support and family preservation services and community based programs. Useful studies already have been done in California (*10 Reasons To Invest in the Families of California*, County Welfare Directors Association of California, Chief Probation Officers Association of California, and California Mental Health Directors Association, 1990) and Missouri (*Where's My Home: A Study of Missouri's Children in Out-of-Home Placement*, Citizens for Missouri's Children, 1989).

- Support legislative initiatives designed to expand and improve income supports, health care, child care, and education for low-income children and families, and those designed to create comprehensive services and support for homeless families with children and families with serious substance abuse problems. These initiatives are critical steps to enabling families to offer better care and support for their children.

VULNERABLE CHILDREN AND FAMILIES
INFORMATION RESOURCES WORKSHEET

Social worker from a local agency: _____

Speaker yes ☐ no ☐   Send materials yes ☐ no ☐   Site visit yes ☐ no ☐

Ask about: needs of children and families served, barriers to serving families, successful prevention and treatment programs, help needed.

Comments/information: _____

_____

_____

Area congregation with program to support vulnerable children: _____

_____

Speaker yes ☐ no ☐   Send materials yes ☐ no ☐   Site visit yes ☐ no ☐

Ask about: program, how established, needs of children and families served, resources contributed by congregation, help needed.

Comments/information: _____

_____

_____

Area foster care/adoption agency: _____

Speaker yes ☐ no ☐   Send materials yes ☐ no ☐   Site visit yes ☐ no ☐

Ask about: special needs of children served, number of children awaiting foster or adoptive families, barriers to placement, help needed.

Comments/information: _____

_____

_____

State child welfare agency: _____

Speaker yes ☐ no ☐   Send materials yes ☐ no ☐

Ask about: trends in abuse and neglect reports and out-of-home placements, special needs of children, barriers to meeting those needs, successful prevention and treatment programs, family preservation service initiatives, help needed.

Comments/information: _____

_____

_____

Statewide or citywide child advocacy group: (look under Children or Social Services in the yellow pages of the phone book)_____

Speaker yes ☐ no ☐   Send materials yes ☐ no ☐
Ask about: its policy or legislative agendas for vulnerable children, new programs and policies which need support, those it hopes to change, barriers to service which need attention, collaboration with other groups, help needed, membership.

Comments/information:_____

_____

_____

Children's Defense Fund, Child Welfare Division, 122 C Street, N.W., Washington, DC 20001, (202) 628-8787.
Send materials yes ☐ no ☐
Ask about: current policy or legislative agendas, innovative policies and programs, help needed.

Comments/information:_____

_____

_____

Child Welfare League of America, 440 First Street, N.W., Suite 310, Washington, DC 20001, (202) 638-2952.
Send materials yes ☐ no ☐
Ask about: current policy or legislative agendas, innovative policies and programs, help needed.

Comments/information:_____

_____

_____

CHAPTER 5:

HOMELESSNESS AND HOUSING

Why are times not kept by the Almighty,
and why do those who know him never see his days?
The wicked remove landmarks;
they seize flocks and pasture them.
They drive away the donkey of the orphan;
they take the widow's ox for a pledge.
They thrust the needy off the road;
the poor of the earth all hide themselves.
Like wild asses in the desert
they go out to their toil,
scavenging in the wasteland
for food for their young.
They reap in a field not their own
and they glean in the vineyard of the wicked.
They lie all night naked, without clothing,
and have no covering in the cold.
They are wet with the rain of the mountains,
and cling to the rock for want of shelter.
There are those who snatch the orphan child from the breast,
and take as a pledge the infant of the poor.
They go about naked, without clothing;
though hungry, they carry the sheaves;
between their terraces, they press out oil;
they tread the wine presses, but suffer thirst.
Job 24:1-11

Children and families represent the single fastest growing population today among America's homeless.
Every day 100,000 American children are homeless.
Children's Defense Fund analyses

And she gave birth to her firstborn son and wrapped him in bands of cloth, and laid him in a manger, because there was no place for them in the inn.
Luke 2:7

"Truly I tell you, just as you did it to one of the least of these who are members of my family, you did it to me."
Matthew 25:40

REFLECTION QUESTIONS

- Read the verse from Luke. Had you ever thought about Jesus as a homeless child before? How does identifying the baby Jesus with homeless people change the picture in your mind as you read this verse?
- Read Matthew 25:34-46. Who were "the least of these" in Jesus' time? Who are they today? Why is it difficult to respond to the needs of people who are homeless?
- Think about the homeless people you see in your community or on the streets of a nearby city. Read Job 24:1-11. How do you connect people who are homeless in our society with this passage? What images of children and families who are homeless might you write in the style of the passage from Job?
- The Israelites often were admonished by the prophets to care for the widows and orphans, those who often were homeless. How do church people today honor that admonition?
- Who pays the highest price for homelessness? What are the costs now and in the future? What are some of the basic needs of children that go unmet when they are homeless?
- What does it mean to be hospitable today? When might we be entertaining angels unaware?
- Think for a moment about Christ's compassion — Christ's *suffering with*, and for, others. Do we tend to feel compassion when encountering a person who is homeless, or do we push our thoughts and feelings away from that close form of identification? What do you think it would be like to be homeless? As a parent with young children? Where would you seek help in your community?

HOMELESSNESS AND HOUSING

Ray is a round-faced boy of 10 who seldom smiles. Until a year ago he and his mother, Jenny, lived in an apartment in San Jose, California. When Jenny, a self-employed auto mechanic, became disabled and was unable to pay the rent, Jenny and Ray were evicted. "We had to sleep by the freeway in the bushes," Ray explains solemnly. "We had a tent."

Now Ray and Jenny live in a shelter for homeless families. When he is asked about his hopes for the future, Ray says he would like to stay in one place and have a friend to play with. He ends his response by saying, "...if I ever get there."

"What do you mean?" the interviewer asks.

"Like I say," says Ray in a flat voice, "tomorrow may never come."

Every night an estimated 100,000 children in this country go to sleep homeless, worrying about what tomorrow will bring. Wondering if tomorrow will come at all.

Homeless families with children are the fastest-growing segment of the homeless population. Our mental pictures of people who are homeless have not caught up fully with that reality. In our mind's eye, many of us see the denizens of Skid Row when we hear about the homeless. But homelessness is not confined to single men, substance abusers, and the mentally ill. The 1980s have produced a rate of homelessness among families far greater than at any time since the Great Depression.

Estimates of the total homeless population range from 250,000 to 3 million. Homeless families with children make up at least one-third of the total. In Kansas City, New York City, and Trenton homeless families make up more than three-quarters of the homeless population. Children in homeless families are spending periods of their crucial childhood years living in cars, in campgrounds, or in crowded, unsanitary, and unsafe public shelters. Many of these children don't eat regularly and don't go to school. They have almost nothing to call their own except anxiety, weariness, and unfilled longings.

Three-year-old Denise lived such a life. For a number of months she spent her nights with her mother, Barbara, and five-year-old brother, James, in a cubicle in a school gym that was used as a homeless shelter in Washington, D.C. Denise was awakened every morning at 5:30 when a staff member pounded on the side of their cubicle. At 7 a.m. a bus took Denise and her family across town to the welfare hotel where they waited for breakfast. After breakfast, the family boarded another bus to take James to a Head Start program. Most days, Denise was tired and cranky because the shelter closed during the day and there was no place for her to take the nap she needed. In the afternoon there was another bus ride to pick up James, dinner at the welfare hotel, and a final bus ride back to the gym.

How has it happened that so many children in America are growing up without a place to call home?

The Low-Income Housing Squeeze

During the 1980s more and more families were caught in the squeeze between high housing costs and inadequate family incomes. Affordable housing for low-income families has been vanishing rapidly in recent years, largely because of drastic Reagan-era budget cuts in federal housing programs. Between 1980 and 1988 federal funding for low-income housing plummeted by more than 80 percent in real dollars. In the late 1970s, about 250,000 low-income housing units were added to our public housing stock each year as a result of federal programs. In 1989 only about 19,000 federally funded housing units were constructed.

Not only has the federal government virtually stopped building public housing, it is not maintaining the existing stock. There are now at least 70,000 units of public housing that cannot be lived in without some degree of renovation, but little federal money is available for repairs.

The loss of public housing units has increased the demand for other low-cost housing and contributed to the general inflation in rents. Between 1970 and 1983 the median rent in this country rose twice as fast as median income, making it increasingly difficult for low-income families to find affordable housing. In Boston, for example, 80 percent of the housing units costing less than $300 a month disappeared between 1982 and 1984, while those renting for more than $600 a month doubled.

While rents have been rising, the number of poor and near-poor families needing low-cost housing has been growing. Between 1980 and 1988 the number of poor families with children increased from fewer than 3.9 million to 5.5 million, a 40 percent rise. Families headed by single women or parents younger than 30 are especially likely to be poor. Single-parent families make up about two-thirds of all homeless families.

Housing experts say that generally no more than 30 percent of a family's gross income should be spent to pay the rent or mortgage and the utility bills. For a family of three earning slightly more than the federal poverty level (about $10,000 a year), that means spending about $250 a month for housing. Yet in 1985 only 8 million housing units at that price were available for the 11.6 million households with incomes below the poverty level.

This huge deficit in the supply of low-cost housing forces millions of low-income families to devote dangerously high proportions of their incomes to rent. In 1985 more than half of all poor renter households spent more than 70 percent of their income on housing. Regardless of

CHILDREN'S DEFENSE FUND

how carefully they budget, these families are always just one crisis away from homelessness. When excessively high rents and low wages prevent families from amassing substantial savings, just one medical emergency, short-term job loss, or other crisis can deplete all financial resources — including money required for rent — and push a family over the edge into homelessness.

Many homeless children fall behind academically because they don't go to school regularly. Children whose families move from place to place never get a chance to settle into one school, and although it is becoming less common, some school districts won't even allow children to enroll without a permanent address or other documents that homeless families often don't have.

When homeless children do go to school they have many strikes against them. Without a quiet place to read or do their homework they find it hard to keep up with their class. They have trouble concentrating because they come to school tired and hungry. Teachers report that homeless students often fall asleep at their desks.

An Agenda for Change

Churches and informal community networks can provide critical help. For example, they can provide short-term loans and emergency food, assist with child care and transportation, or offer decent temporary shelter. Church organizations can make sure that homeless families have access to existing social services such as health care and welfare. And churches can mobilize the community to provide people who are homeless with specialized services that are not available elsewhere, such as help with job and housing searches.

As necessary as these efforts are, they will never solve the root problem, however. Families are homeless because there is a huge shortage of permanent low-cost housing. More than anything else, homeless families need housing they can afford. Although the private sector can and should make significant contributions toward alleviating the low-cost housing shortage, the private sector cannot solve the problem by itself.

Since the Depression some poor families have received housing assistance through subsidized rental housing, but there has been a great imbalance between government assistance in the form of tax deductions to homeowners, who are primarily middle- and upper-income people, and government assistance to low-income renters. Today the federal government appropriates about $10 billion each year for low-income housing assistance. In contrast, the federal government forgoes about $53 billion in tax revenue each year by giving significant tax breaks to homeowners.

The federal and state governments must invest more money in effective programs for building and rehabilitating public housing. As concerned citizens, we must tell our elected officials that we support programs to increase the stock of decent public housing.

WHAT CAN YOU DO ABOUT THE NEEDS OF CHILDREN AND FAMILIES WHO ARE HOMELESS OR HAVE INADEQUATE HOUSING?

Educate Yourself and Others

- Read articles in newspapers and denominational publications about homelessness and inadequate housing. Education is the first step toward compassion.
- Invite local housing advocates to speak to groups or open committee meetings for your congregation.
- Include basic facts about homelessness locally and nationally in your church newsletter or a worship bulletin insert.
- Develop programs for children and youths to raise their awareness of the housing problem. Many children who are homeless avoid school because they are treated cruelly by other children.
- Visit or spend a night in a shelter for homeless people.

Get Involved in Meeting the Need

- Ask your congregation to support a shelter for homeless families by providing volunteers, clothing, bedding, food, or money.
- Create an emergency fund. Contributions can provide one-time grants or no-interest loans to pay back rent, security deposits, or utility payments. Grants or loans of this type can keep families from losing their homes or help homeless families secure housing.
- Assist a homeless family or a family on the brink of homelessness. Through your congregation, provide assistance directly to a family known by your pastor. You also can work through a religious or public social service agency. Families may need help with child care, job leads, finding a place to live, or furniture. They may simply need to have someone in their lives who cares. This kind of support and assistance can prevent homelessness and help homeless families regain stability in permanent housing.
- Develop respite care programs for families living in homeless shelters. Include homeless children and youths in existing day care, religious education, and other ministries of your congregation. Recruit members of the congregation to provide child care and recreation for homeless children while their parents in-

terview for jobs, attend worship, or seek permanent housing.

- Help develop housing for low-income families. Many congregations have joined with nonprofit organizations and local governments to construct and rehabilitate low-income housing. Your congregation actually can be the developer and builder, or can provide financial and personnel support to other groups, such as Habitat for Humanity International (Habitat and Church Streets, Americus, GA 31709, 912-924-6935).

Advocate for Homeless Children and Families

- Tell local, state, and federal officials about the homeless families in your area. Urge them to make housing assistance available to all who need help and a priority for government funds. Also, urge them to increase AFDC benefits and the minimum wage to levels that will allow low-income families to afford decent and safe housing.
- Develop a program you can take to community groups to enlist their help in providing adequate housing in your area.
- Join with others to sponsor a Children's Awareness Tour. Arrange visits with public and private agencies concerned with homeless children and families. Invite business and religious leaders, public officials, and members of the press.
- Find out if homeless children are getting the health care and education services to which they are entitled. If not, find out why, and advocate for changes.

WHAT YOUNG PEOPLE CAN DO TO HELP HOMELESS CHILDREN

Always treat homeless children the way you would want to be treated. It is very hard and sometimes very embarrassing to be homeless. Try to imagine what it would be like. Talk about it with your classmates.

- What would you do after school?
- How would it feel not to sleep in your own bed?
- Which of your things (clothes, toys, books) would you choose if you could only keep what you could carry yourself?
- What would it be like to eat all your meals in a cafeteria or soup kitchen and not be able to choose your favorite foods?
- What would it be like to have to miss a lot of school or change schools many times?

Ask your parents or teachers to help you find community organizations or churches that are helping homeless people. Here are some things you, your classmates, and your family can do to help such organizations:

- You can work in a soup kitchen, serving food to children and adults. Homeless people often don't get enough to eat, and soup kitchens offer them free meals.
- You can help a church or other group collect money to help people pay their rent so they don't get kicked out of their homes. Sometimes just a little bit of money can help people keep their homes.
- Collect clothes that you and other people in your family don't wear anymore. Give them to a shelter for homeless people. Many homeless children and adults lose clothing when they become homeless and often don't have the money to replace it.
- Ask someone who works with homeless children and adults to come talk to your class about the people they work with and the problems homeless families face.
- Ask a person who works with homeless children and adults about other kinds of things you can do to help them.
- Write letters to the city council in your town and to national politicians, including the president, your senators, and representatives, and ask them what they are doing to help homeless people. (Officials' addresses are in the phone book.)

HOMELESSNESS AND HOUSING
INFORMATION RESOURCES WORKSHEET

Local family shelter:_____

Speaker yes ☐ no ☐   Send materials yes ☐ no ☐   Site visit yes ☐ no ☐

Ask about: type of shelter, number served, number on waiting list, number of those served who are children, needs, resources, etc.

Comments/information: _____

_____

_____

Area church with program to serve homeless children and families: _____

Speaker yes ☐ no ☐   Send materials yes ☐ no ☐   Site visit yes ☐ no ☐

Ask about: process to establish program, how it works, problems, needs, number served and the trend over time, costs, etc.

Comments/information: _____

_____

_____

Local housing authority:_____

Speaker yes ☐ no ☐   Send materials yes ☐ no ☐

Ask about: number of subsidized housing units, policy on affordable housing development, number on waiting list. Also ask about policy on emergency shelters, number on waiting list. You may need to call a separate office for public housing and other subsidies.

Comments/information: _____

_____

_____

State or local agency for homelessness assistance: _____

Speaker yes ☐ no ☐   Send materials yes ☐ no ☐

Ask about: policy on homelessness, shelters; prevention programs, services.

Comments/information: _____

_____

_____

Statewide housing/homeless advocacy group: _____
(look for Habitat for Humanity chapter, or Low-Income Housing Coalition or Coalition for the Homeless in the phone book)

Speaker yes ☐ no ☐   Send materials yes ☐ no ☐

Ask about: membership, action agenda, etc.

Comments/information: _____
_____
_____

Children's Defense Fund, Homelessness/Housing Division, 122 C Street, N.W., Washington, DC 20001, (202) 628-8787.

Send materials yes ☐ no ☐

Ask about: current agenda, legislative items, desired actions.

Comments/information: _____
_____
_____

Interagency Council on the Homeless, 451 7th Street, S.W., Room 7274, Washington, DC 20410, (202) 708-1480. (Executive branch agency.)

Send materials yes ☐ no ☐

Ask about: current policy and programs to assist homeless children and families, including information on access to health and education resources for homeless children, homelessness prevention programs, income support, statistics and trends over time for number of homeless children and families.

Express concern/interest in: supporting policies and programs that prevent homelessness and help homeless people.

Comments/information: _____
_____
_____

Chapter 6:

MATERNAL AND CHILD HEALTH

Thus says the Lord:
A voice is heard in Ramah,
    lamentation and bitter weeping.
Rachel is weeping for her children,
    she refuses to be comforted for her children,
    because they are no more.

Jeremiah 31:15

Each year, nearly 40,000 babies in the United States die before their first birthday. Another 400,000 develop a chronic or disabling condition....Infant death and disability are *not* intractable problems. This country has the knowledge necessary to save 10,000 additional infant lives each year and to prevent an untold number of disabilities among infants. To do that, we as a nation must apply what we know about illness prevention and health promotion and ensure that the women at greatest risk of having an unhealthy baby have access to high-quality primary health and social services.

Report of the White House Task Force on Infant Mortality

There is no finer investment for any community than putting milk into babies.

Sir Winston Churchill

Suddenly a leader of the synagogue came in and knelt before [Jesus], saying, "My daughter has just died; but come and lay your hand on her, and she will live." And Jesus got up and followed him, with his disciples....When Jesus got to the leader's house and saw the flute players and the crowd making a commotion, he said, "Go away; for the girl is not dead but sleeping." And they laughed at him. But when the crowd had been put outside, he went in and took her by the hand, and the girl got up. And the report of this spread throughout that district.

Matthew 9:18-19, 23-26

REFLECTION QUESTIONS

- The passage from Jeremiah refers to Rachel, the mother of Joseph and Benjamin, who is lamenting their exile. The verse introduces the promise of the restoration of the kingdoms and the return from exile. This verse is also quoted in Matthew (2:18) to depict unrelieved grief. Which setting fits our world? What is the grief we have for the health of children? What is the promise or hope in the future?

- How do you interpret the last two lines of the poem by Gabriela Mistral found in Section I on page 27? Note the facts presented above this quote. What does the poet mean by "The child's name is `Today'"? Why is investing in the health of pregnant women, infants, and children such an urgent concern?

- The healing story from Matthew is one of a few stories in the gospels that includes children in an obvious way. It is significant because a child is healed. In the middle of this gospel story is the healing of a woman. This, too, is significant, for Jesus has taken special notice of these two of the powerless in Jewish society. How might you connect this story with a national concern for maternal and child health?

- As a society, what is our responsibility when children die of preventable causes? How would you characterize the moral cost to our society? How does this problem affect your life or that of your family?

MATERNAL AND CHILD HEALTH

The United States is one of the richest nations and perhaps the most medically advanced nation in the world. Yet by some measures this country is still underdeveloped when it comes to keeping our children healthy. The infant mortality rates for black babies in Boston, Los Angeles, and Chicago, for example, are about the same as those in Trinidad and Tobago.

This is a shocking fact, for the United States spends fully 11 percent of its gross national product on health care. Every month we hear about new breakthroughs in medical research, new miracle drugs, and new surgical procedures. We assume that American children are getting the best health care modern medicine can provide, which may be true for children covered by health insurance.

However, more than 9 million American children — one in seven — had no health insurance of any kind in 1988. In addition, more than 14 million American women in their prime childbearing years either were completely uninsured or were uninsured for maternity care.

The great majority of uninsured women and children live in low-income working families. More and more people work for employers who don't offer health benefits or who don't pay the cost of their employees' family health coverage. The proportion of medium-size and large employers paying the full cost of family health care coverage has shrunk by one-third in the past decade.

Medicaid is the federally funded program that finances health care for welfare families and hundreds of thousands of low-income pregnant women and millions of children in other low-income families. But Medicaid does not begin to pay for health care for all the low-income children who are not covered by private health insurance. For example, in 1990 children age seven and older living in families with incomes above state welfare eligibility levels could not be covered by Medicaid. This left out millions of poor school-age children and adolescents.

Low-income families without Medicaid or private health insurance must rely on public hospitals and a patchwork system of public health clinics that is underfunded and understaffed to meet these families' needs. Some rural areas don't have any public health clinics at all, and for-profit hospitals often try to avoid serving low-income families. Some private hospitals, for example, don't list phone numbers for their emergency rooms in the phone book; many hospitals won't admit someone who doesn't have insurance and appears unlikely to be able to pay the bill. Some hospitals have turned away pregnant women only minutes away from giving birth or children in comas because they could not pay.

The amount and quality of health care an American child receives has very little to do with what is necessary to keep him or her healthy. It has almost everything to do with the child's family income, whether he or she happens to live near a public health clinic, and the state's eligibility requirements for Medicaid.

Poor Health Begins Before Birth...

The health problems of poor children often originate before birth because many low-income mothers can't afford adequate prenatal care. Women who don't see a doctor regularly while they are pregnant are more likely to have infants born at low birthweight — weighing less than 5.5 pounds. If they live, these tiny babies are likely to suffer from serious problems such as mental retardation, cerebral palsy, and vision and learning disabilities. But many don't live. Low-birthweight babies are six times more likely than average-weight babies to die during their first month of life, and three times more likely to die before their first birthday.

In fact, low birthweight is the leading cause of infant mortality in this country. Compared with other industrialized nations, the overall U.S. infant mortality rate (the number of deaths of babies younger than one year for every 1,000 live births) is very high. Our rate of 10.4 places the United States eighteenth in the world, behind all the industrialized European nations, and even behind Singapore and Hong Kong.

The U.S. statistics are even more shocking when our infant mortality rate for black infants is compared with overall rates in other nations. In 1988 the United States ranked twenty-eighth, behind Cuba, Bulgaria, and Czechoslovakia, and tied with Poland, Hungary, Portugal, and Costa Rica.

...and Continues Through Childhood

One way to get an idea of how well a nation is taking care of its toddlers and preschool children is to look at immunization rates, since young children who have regular medical checkups are almost sure to be immunized against preventable childhood diseases such as diphtheria, polio, measles, mumps, and whooping cough.

By this measure, the United States clearly is failing to protect the health of growing numbers of children, for during the first half of the 1980s the proportion of immunized two-year-olds began to drop. In 1980 almost 81 percent of all two-year-olds were immunized against polio, for example. Five years later, the proportion had decreased to 77 percent.

Ten years ago the United States was on the verge of eradicating measles, but the drop in immunization rates among preschool children has caused a new measles epidemic. Between 1983 and 1989 the number of measles cases increased 1,000 percent. More than 20,000 measles cases and 60 measles deaths were reported in just the first eight months of 1990.

Other measures also tell the story of inadequate health care for many poor children. Low-income children are more than three times as likely as other children never to have had a preventive health exam, and one in five never sees a doctor in the course of a year. Anemia, which slows physical development and makes it hard for children to pay attention in school, is three times more common in poor children than in other children. Hearing loss from untreated ear infections is also more common.

Health Care Is a Good Investment

At a time when the national budget deficit is on everyone's mind, people of all political persuasions are arguing that, despite the need, the United States can't afford to spend more money on health care. That argument is tragically shortsighted.

First, our nation does not really save money by scrimping on preventive health care, because the cost of emergency care and rehabilitation is far greater than the cost of prevention. For example, it costs about $150 to immunize a child fully against preventable disease, but it costs on average more than $600 a day to hospitalize a child for a case of measles or whooping cough that could have been prevented with vaccines. Children who receive ongoing pediatric care through Medicaid and other publicly financed programs have annual health care costs that are nearly 10 percent lower than children who do not have ongoing care. And while maternity care for a woman costs about $5,000, the average bill for 20 days of intensive neonatal care for a low-birthweight infant is more than $20,000.

Second, there are many hidden costs associated with poor health. Unhealthy children have a hard time learning, and learning problems often lead to delinquency, dropping out of school, and unemployment. Our nation loses a great deal of potential talent, productive work, and tax dollars as a result of the diminished productivity of adults who were physically or educationally disabled by preventable causes during childhood.

Complete nutrition for pregnant women and children is a cornerstone of good health. The Special Supplemental Food Program for Women, Infants, and Children (WIC) can provide the extra food and advice needed by low-income families. Each $1 spent through WIC to provide nutrition and support services to a pregnant woman saves $3 in the first year of a child's life by reducing low-birthweight births and prematurity. One key to the success of WIC is that it not only provides better nutrition, but a link to prenatal care as well.

Despite its effectiveness, WIC currently is not federally funded at a sufficient level to serve all of the eligible pregnant women and young children. In virtually every state the WIC program has a waiting list of women, infants, and children who need food supplements.

An Agenda for Change

Our nation has a long way to go before all American children receive the basic health care they need, regardless of their parents' income. No child or pregnant woman should be without an accessible doctor or clinic and health insurance. Until all pregnant women and children have universal health insurance coverage, Congress must expand Medicaid to reach all pregnant women and children younger than 19 whose family income is less than twice the federal poverty level — about $20,000 per year for a family of three. In addition, the president and Congress should expand programs that put physicians, clinics, and basic health services where they are needed. These programs include the Childhood Immunization Program, the National Health Service Corps, and Community and Migrant Health Centers.

Most low-income families don't need high-tech medicine, but they do need a health care system that does the following:

- Widely advertises its services;
- Has many easy-to-reach providers, and offers transportation assistance in rural areas to those who need it;
- Has employees who are responsive to special community needs, including bilingual staff, staff trained to work with families with low levels of literacy, and staff trained to serve persons with disabilities;
- Keeps eligibility requirements and application procedures simple;
- Provides comprehensive services promptly and in centralized locations; and
- Has medical and administrative personnel who understand the socioeconomic aspects of health issues, who are committed to being health educators, and who take the time to make sure patients understand the prescribed treatment and how it relates to their complaints.

Third, the WIC program, which currently serves only about half of the estimated eligible population, should have sufficient federal funding to allow nutritional support to all poor and nutritionally at-risk women, infants, and children who apply. As well, every state should follow the example of the approximately one dozen states that use their funds to supplement federal WIC dollars, and that use their purchasing power to secure competitive bids and reduce infant formula prices.

As concerned citizens we must make sure our elected officials and community leaders know that we support policies and programs that ensure basic health care for all infants, children, and pregnant women. In addition, we can offer various kinds of assistance to help community clinics and health care programs do a better job of serving low-income families.

WHAT CAN YOU DO TO MEET THE NEEDS FOR MATERNAL AND CHILD HEALTH CARE?

Educate Yourself and Others

- Invite a representative from your city or county health department, WIC program, or a community health clinic to speak to your congregation or a group within it about the health needs of pregnant women and children in your area.
- Write a letter to the editor of your local newspaper about the unmet health needs of women and children in your area and encourage strong local action.
- Create a chart that shows the health services available to people at various economic levels of your community. Display it in your church building. Distribute copies of it to other congregations and community groups.

Get Involved in the Community

- Organize volunteers to transport pregnant women and parents and children to and from local health clinics that provide prenatal and pediatric care. Work with clinics to advertise the availability of the free transportation and to schedule it at appropriate times.
- Set up and staff a play area in a health clinic or WIC program office for children waiting with family members.
- Donate congregational space for prenatal care classes whenever the courses are needed. Encourage women from the congregation to take part in staffing or attending the courses.
- Give a community baby shower to educate pregnant women about the need for prenatal care and to provide them with baby clothing and other necessary items.
- Adopt a health clinic — much like the "adopt a school" program — and provide financial support, volunteers, and help with community relations.
- Work with local, public, and religious-affiliated hospitals to develop arrangements that will enable pregnant women who lack health insurance to get hospital care for their deliveries.
- Donate congregational space for immunization clinics. Weekend and evening clinics can help working families have access to services. Encourage congregation members to take part in staffing these clinics.
- Volunteer time to accompany public health nurses or social workers. Members of congregations, especially those located in inner city areas, could use a buddy system to assist public health staff making home visits to pregnant women and mothers.

Advocate for Adequate Maternal and Child Health Care

- Help generate business and corporate support for community groups working to improve the health of infants and children.
- Join a local or state coalition of groups and individuals that seeks to improve the health status of children and pregnant women by removing financial barriers to care, increasing access to health services, and educating the public about available health services.
- Organize health care professionals within your own congregation or help area congregations take a more visible and active role in educating, volunteering, and advocating on behalf of at-risk pregnant women, infants, and children.
- Help educate policy makers at the federal, state, and local levels. Write to elected officials, outlining your concerns and advocating for preventive, cost-effective investments in the health of today's children.
- Help educate community leaders and policy makers by organizing visits to public clinics, hospital neonatal intensive care units, and WIC program sites.

MATERNAL AND CHILD HEALTH
INFORMATION RESOURCES WORKSHEET

Local health clinic/neighborhood health center: (ask for the medical director or head of clinical staff)

_____

Speaker yes ☐ no ☐   Send materials yes ☐ no ☐   Site visit yes ☐ no ☐

Ask about: number of uninsured children and pregnant women, most critical health problems, types of maternal and child health care services offered (e.g. prenatal care, preventive health care, services for children with special health needs), whether women and children are able to enroll in Medicaid on-site, and need for volunteer assistance.

Comments/information:_____

_____

_____

Local public, community, or children's hospital: (ask for chief of obstetrics or pediatrics) _____

Speaker yes ☐ no ☐   Send materials yes ☐ no ☐   Site visit yes ☐ no ☐

Ask about: proportion of children and pregnant women admitted who are uninsured, whether other facilities for the uninsured are available, and types of preventable conditions that hospitalized children have.

Comments/information:_____

_____

_____

City/county health department: (ask for agency head's office) _____

Speaker yes ☐ no ☐   Send materials yes ☐ no ☐

Ask about: county/city statistics for uninsured children, infant mortality, proportion of low-birthweight babies, childhood immunization, WIC funding and numbers.

Comments/information:_____

_____

_____

State maternal and child health (MCH) agency: (contact state agency head, who is located in the state health department)_____

Speaker yes ☐ no ☐   Send materials yes ☐ no ☐

Ask about: statewide statistics on infant mortality and low birthweight, immunization; proportion of children with disabilities; proportion of children who are uninsured; WIC funding and proportion of eligible women, infants, and children served.

Comments/information:_____

_____

_____

State Medicaid agency: (ask for director's office — usually part of state welfare or health agency _____

Speaker yes ☐ no ☐   Send materials yes ☐ no ☐

Ask about: whether all pregnant women and infants with incomes below 185 percent of poverty level are covered, proportion of children under age six who receive Medicaid's Early and Periodic Screening, Diagnosis, and Treatment (EPSDT) program benefits, proportion of children ages six to 20 who receive EPSDT benefits, whether women and children can enroll in Medicaid at area health clinics and neighborhood health centers, proportion of state pediatricians who treat Medicaid patients, and proportion of obstetricians who treat Medicaid patients.

Comments/information:_____

_____

_____

Statewide health advocacy organization: (call CDF Health Division, state MCH agency, or state legal services program

for contact suggestions) _____

Speaker yes ☐ no ☐   Send materials yes ☐ no ☐

Ask about: major issues on which the organization works and any available reports and statistics.

Comments/information:_____

_____

_____

Children's Defense Fund, Health Division, 122 C Street, N.W., Washington, DC 20001, (202) 628-8787.

Send materials yes ☐ no ☐

Ask about: current agenda, legislative items, and desired actions.

Comments/information:_____

_____

_____

CHAPTER 7:

YOUTH SELF-SUFFICIENCY AND TEEN PREGNANCY PREVENTION

But now hear, O Jacob my servant,
    Israel whom I have chosen!
Thus says the Lord who made you,
    who formed you in the womb and will help you;
Do not fear, O Jacob my servant,
    Jeshurun whom I have chosen.
For I will pour water on the thirsty land,
    and streams on the dry ground.
I will pour my spirit upon your descendants,
    and my blessing on your offspring.
They shall spring up like a green tamarisk,
    like willows by flowing streams.

Isaiah 44:1-4

May our sons in their youth
    be like plants full grown,
our daughters like corner pillars,
    cut for the building of a palace.

Psalm 144:12

Let no one despise your youth, but set the believers an example in speech and conduct, in love, in faith, in purity. Until I arrive, give attention to the public reading of scripture, to exhorting, to teaching. Do not neglect the gift that is in you.

1 Timothy 4:12-14

The United States' teen pregnancy rate is twice as high as that of other industrialized countries. Before the age of 20, two in five American girls get pregnant and one in five American girls bears a child.

Children's Defense Fund analysis

Children almost never do what we say but almost always do what we do.

James Baldwin

REFLECTION QUESTIONS

- What is the prevalent attitude toward young people in these biblical quotes? How is that attitude manifested in your congregation? How is it ignored?
- As you think about the teenagers in your congregation and community, what words or images come to your mind? How many of your congregation's youths do you know by name?
- If you were writing a psalm of praise to God for young people, what would you say? What images would you use to express what you hope for the young people?
- What kind of an environment, or what supports, do the sons and daughters of our nation need to flourish "like plants full grown" and to be as solid and stable as "corner pillars of a palace"? What kind of education, job preparation, and information on issues related to sexuality and family life do they need?

YOUTH SELF-SUFFICIENCY AND
TEEN PREGNANCY PREVENTION

What kind of future do we want for the teenagers we love? We want them to become adults who are capable of establishing healthy, fulfilling lives for themselves. We want them to be well-educated, to have jobs they enjoy and incomes that will support a home and a family. We want them to become nurturing parents and citizens who contribute to their community.

We work hard to provide the material, emotional, and spiritual resources to help our own teenagers achieve such a future. But there are far too many teenagers in our communities who are not receiving the support and guidance they need to make a successful transition from adolescence to adulthood.

"I'm 18 years of age," writes a young woman who lives in one of Chicago's public housing projects. "I have one little girl and one on the way, which truthfully I don't want. I've been expelled from high school when I was just about to complete my senior year. I'm also unemployed."

Early pregnancy and parenthood are both symptoms and causes of an adolescence that offers few positive options for the future. So are drug and alcohol abuse, crime, school dropout, low academic achievement, and unemployment. All these "rotten outcomes," as author Lisbeth Schorr calls them, tell us that families, churches, schools, and other community groups are falling short in preparing our most vulnerable teenagers for healthy, productive lives as workers, citizens, and parents. The Carnegie Council on Adolescent Development estimates that about one-quarter, or 7 million, of the 28 million U.S. youngsters between the ages of 10 and 17 are at serious risk of school failure, substance abuse, and teen pregnancy and parenthood. Another 7 million are at moderate risk.

The Causes of Too-Early Parenthood

Social scientists know a great deal about the conditions that lead to school failure, adolescent crime, drug and alcohol abuse, and teenage pregnancy. These risks are closely related to premature birth or low birthweight, poor health, family stress, inadequate schools, and the lack of close relationships with loving adults. The children most likely to face such risks are those who grow up in poverty.

Poor children get a weak start in life even before they are born. Poor parents are less likely to have access to adequate prenatal care, meaning that their babies are at increased risk of being born at low birthweight, a condition associated with a number of serious mental and physical handicaps, including learning disabilities.

As they grow up, poor children are less likely to receive key building blocks of early development — adequate nutrition, good medical care, and a safe, stimulating environment. Children who are ill, undernourished, or undernurtured are often less alert, less curious, and interact less effectively with their environment than do other children.

Poor children are also more likely to live with parents who themselves did poorly in school, dropped out, and lack job skills. One illiterate father told writer Jonathan Kozol: "My son was supposed to repeat ninth grade for the third time this year. He finally said he wanted to drop out. I see my handicap being passed on to my son. I tell you, it scares me."

As a society we could help poor children compensate for their disadvantages by making sure they went to the best schools with the most skillful teachers. Instead, poor children generally go to the worst schools, where chunks of ceiling and walls are missing, bathrooms do not work, windows are permanently boarded up, and the teachers are tired and indifferent.

Girls who grow up craving love, who have little sense of self-worth and no dreams for the future, are likely to feel they have nothing to offer but their bodies and not much to lose if they get pregnant. Carrying a baby may be the only achievement they think they have a realistic shot at. Says one young mother, "It's the one time in my life I really felt like I'm *somebody*, like I'm doing something. People come around and expect me to feel ashamed of myself but instead I feel proud of myself, like I can at least make a baby."

As for disadvantaged boys, they may be particularly likely to view the initiation of sexual activity as the marker of adulthood. Low-income youths generally lack the family expectations and life scripts that point to other benchmarks of progress toward adulthood and provide motivation for delaying sexual activity. Without other points of reference that confirm their increasing status, disadvantaged teenage boys are likely to have considerable stake in sexual activity and the ability to become a parent.

The Disastrous Consequences of
Too-Early Parenthood

Even if the life experiences of many teenagers have not taught them the wisdom of avoiding too-early parenthood, the disastrous consequences are increasingly apparent:

- In a high-tech economy, the lack of at least a high school diploma is an increasingly serious barrier to economic self-sufficiency. Yet half of all young women who give birth before age 18 do not obtain a high school diploma by their mid-twenties, and a disproportionate number of young fathers drop out of school, as well.

- Two incomes are increasingly necessary to maintain a young family above the poverty line, but most teen mothers raise their children alone. Sixty percent of teen births are to unmarried mothers.

CHILDREN'S DEFENSE FUND

- In 1987 almost two-thirds of all children younger than three who lived in families headed by a parent younger than 22 were poor. The baby of a single black mother younger than 22 has an almost 100 percent chance of being poor.

Early childbearing jeopardizes the future of both the parents and the children. But it is not merely a personal issue. Because the vicious cycle of too-early parenthood, poverty, and too-early parenthood in the next generation deprives the nation of educated, productive workers, it has serious implications for the nation's economic future.

What Teenagers Need To Prevent Pregnancy: Positive Life Options

In 1981 New York industrialist-philanthropist Eugene Lang made an impulsive offer to a class of graduating sixth-graders at the Harlem elementary school from which he had graduated 50 years earlier. He promised the 59 black and Latino students he would pay for a college education for every one of them who graduated from high school.

Before too long, however, Lang realized that the goal of a college education lacked reality for children living in an environment where educational achievement was not stressed and long-range life planning was a rarity. Lang saw that if he was going to make a positive difference in the lives of these sixth-graders, he needed to do more than hold out the distant promise of a college education and take them on an occasional museum visit.

So Lang and an associate, working in conjunction with a community action agency in East Harlem, set about building a continuous support system for his adopted students. Every day for six years Lang's students received an array of personal and academic supports that helped them get through high school. By January 1988, 48 of the original 59 students had graduated — in an environment where the dropout rate is as high as 50 percent.

Lang's I Have a Dream program demonstrates that high-risk adolescents can work toward a promising future if they receive early, intensive, comprehensive, personalized help. No one foundation, social service program, school system, or community group can provide the full range of supports that disadvantaged students need. But working together, communities and schools can offer teenagers experiences that will increase their stake in the future and their opportunities for choosing a constructive life path.

Disadvantaged teens need what all teenagers need. Among other things, these are:
- Caring relationships with adults who can give counsel and support at critical turning points and serve as positive role models.
- Recreation programs, hobbies, and other activities that integrate them into the community and build

confidence and self-esteem.
- Opportunities to talk about and set goals for the future that offer realistic alternatives to life-limiting behavior such as pregnancy, drug and alcohol abuse, and dropping out of school.
- School-to-work programs that lead to meaningful employment for those who do not go on to postsecondary education.
- Consciousness-raising about the consequences of too-early sexual activity and parenthood, and access to health care services that address their developing sexuality and the emotional vulnerabilities of adolescence.

It's important to begin offering youngsters these life-enhancing experiences during early adolescence, *before* they drift onto the paths where pregnancy and parenthood, drug use, and dropping out of school "just happen." Since the growth and change that occur in youngsters between the ages of about 10 and 15 is greater than the change occurring in any other phase of life except infancy, the experiences children have during these vulnerable years are vitally important to their development. For many disadvantaged children, these years represent their last and best chance to choose a path that will lead to a fulfilling, productive life; yet our schools and community services have tended to ignore this age group.

Fears that increased information and accessible contraceptive services will increase sexual activity among teens are not supported by the evidence. There is evidence that better access to information and contraceptive services at school health clinics, for example, may encourage girls to postpone sexual activity. In a Baltimore demonstration program, the proportion of girls who became sexually active by age 14 went down by 40 percent after a teen health clinic was established, and the median age at which girls began sexual activity rose by seven months.

The double standard for girls and boys continues to be one of the most serious threats to efforts to help teens delay sexual activity. Since young men generally are not as interested as young women in sexuality-specific services and programs, motivating boys to prevent pregnancy requires innovative approaches that integrate sex education into other activities. These approaches include:
- Taking the message and the service to the places and programs where young men congregate.
- Adding a sex education component to other kinds of programs and services that attract young men, such as employment and training programs, recreation programs, and athletic programs.
- Making sure that programs and services are offered by adults with whom teenage boys can identify and in surroundings in which they feel comfortable.

The supports, experiences, and opportunities we want for our own teenagers are exactly what we must give *all* teenagers. We must be advocates in our communities and our states for public policies and programs that provide teenagers with the services they need to become happy, productive adults. But even more, we must contribute our own time and efforts to community programs that give teenagers a real stake in their own futures.

WHAT CAN YOU DO TO HEIGHTEN OPPORTUNITIES FOR YOUTHS?

Educate Yourself and Others

- Talk with young people in your neighborhood or congregation to hear what they need and want. Arrange intergenerational activities for young people and adults to meet and get to know one another.
- Survey the counseling resources for young people in your community. How does your congregation support them? Do the youths of your congregation feel they can draw on the church for confidential guidance and support? How can you convey the availability of that counsel?
- Create a bulletin board of youth-serving agencies and services, including information and referral to accessible and affordable health facilities, counseling, and academic and vocational training sites.

Get Involved in Meeting the Needs of Young People

- Offer communication workshops for parents and teens, programs on alcohol and other drugs, and peer group or intergenerational discussions on human sexuality and teen pregnancy issues.
- Talk with an adult church school group or fellowship group about being mentors to young people in your congregation or the community. Check with local schools to see if such a program is in place, or contact the Big Brothers and Big Sisters organization in your area.
- With young people, set up an employment service for teens to do odd jobs for people in the congregation and community. This can help them develop good work habits as well as earn money.
- Develop a community service program or project run by disadvantaged teens to encourage their sense of being needed and of having something to give.

- Acknowledge the achievements of the young people in your congregation when they receive awards, scholarships, are graduated, or enter new schools.
- Set up a scholarship fund to help young people go to college or training institutions.
- Work with community institutions and organizations to create systems of support for at-risk teens, pregnant and parenting teens, unemployed youths, and homeless young people. Volunteer to help in the schools that the young people attend, or in youth programs in your congregation or community.
- Make your church available after school and in the evenings for structured recreational activities for youths, and tutorial and special enrichment programs. Use your church van to transport young people to periodic cultural events and recreational activities.

Advocate for Young People in Your Community

- Write to elected officials informing them of the unmet needs you have discovered. Urge them to look into the needs of young people in your area and around the nation, and recommend a course of action.
- Help the young people participate in advocacy for themselves. Hold a voter registration project in cooperation with the high school student council. Arrange to use a real voting machine to familiarize teens with the actual process.
- Ask the program chairpersons of professional, business, or service groups of which you are a member to schedule at least one meeting in the coming year to learn of ways they can help young people who are at risk.
- Work with the local high school to offer a school-to-work program through which professionals from your congregation offer internships to students, particularly those at risk.

CHILDREN'S DEFENSE FUND

YOUTH DEVELOPMENT AND TEEN PREGNANCY PREVENTION INFORMATION RESOURCES WORKSHEET

Local program serving teens: (look under Youth Programs or Community Organizations in the phone book, or for local branch of the United Way, Boys and Girls Clubs, YMCA, or YWCA)

_____

Speaker yes ☐ no ☐   Send materials yes ☐ no ☐   Site visit yes ☐ no ☐

Ask about: most critical problems facing area teens (e.g. runaways, teen pregnancy, dropping out, etc.), services provided, who is the population being served, resources and needs, and gaps in local services.

Comments/information: _____

_____

_____

Area church with outreach program to teens: _____

Speaker yes ☐ no ☐   Send materials yes ☐ no ☐   Site visit yes ☐ no ☐

Ask about: how program meets needs, how established, resources, needs, services provided, population served.

Comments/information: _____

_____

_____

Local social service agency serving teens: (look in the phone book under Social Services or Family Services, and in government section under those categories in addition to Health and Recreation Departments)

_____

Speaker yes ☐ no ☐   Send materials yes ☐ no ☐

Ask about: most critical problems facing area teens, most successful programs, goals for program or policy changes, and gaps in local services.

Comments/information: _____

_____

_____

State-level agency for adolescent policies and programs: (start by calling the governor's office and state health department)_____

Speaker yes ☐ no ☐   Send materials yes ☐ no ☐

Ask about: most critical problems facing teens in your state, trends in population in need and in population served, most successful programs and policies, program or policy areas needing improvement.

Comments/information: _____

_____

_____

Statewide advocacy group: (ask the above contacts; or the Children's Defense Fund, Youth Development Division)

Speaker yes ☐ no ☐   Send materials yes ☐ no ☐

Ask about: relevant statistics regarding teens in your state — what is the dropout rate, teen pregnancy rate, etc.; legislative and administrative agenda and desired actions; membership information.

Comments/information: _____

_____

_____

Children's Defense Fund, Education, Adolescent Pregnancy Prevention, and Youth Development Division, 122 C Street, N.W., Washington, DC 20001, (202) 628-8787.

Speaker yes ☐ no ☐   Send materials yes ☐ no ☐

Ask about: Child Watch groups in your area, current legislative items, desired actions, relevant statistics regarding teens in your state, successful program models, and research reports.

Comments/information: _____

_____

_____

The Alan Guttmacher Institute, 360 Park Avenue, New York, NY 10003, (212) 254-5656.
Ask about: policies it supports, model programs, and publications and other sources of information.

Association of Junior Leagues, Inc., 825 Third Avenue, 27th Floor, New York, NY 10022, (212) 355-4380.
Ask about: their school-based pregnancy prevention Teen Outreach Program (TOP).

Center for Population Options, 1012 14th Street, N.W., Washington, DC 20005, (202) 347-5700.
Ask about: policies it supports; model programs; periodicals, fact sheets, and other publications related to adolescent pregnancy and prevention.

National Organization on Adolescent Pregnancy and Parenting, P.O. Box 2365, Reston, VA 22090, (703) 435-2365.
Ask about: its national membership-based network, resources, newsletter.

GIVING VOICE TO THE VOICELESS

INTRODUCTION

Speak out for those who cannot speak, for the rights of all the destitute. Speak out, judge righteously, defend the rights of the needy.

Proverbs 31:8-9

S peaking out for fair public policies for children is a vital part of child advocacy and one in which the Children's Defense Fund has taken a leading role. Such work is an appropriate and important extension of Christian worship and study, as well. Our study of scripture reveals to us a God who cares deeply for those who are without power. It further reveals a faith not meant to be compartmentalized or limited to Sunday worship, but rather to be lived and acted upon throughout all aspects of our lives. Advocating for public policies that benefit children and families is one vital way that we can embody God's love for others.

This section of the book is designed to help you advocate for children in the political arena. **Chapter 1: Why Should We Raise Our Voices?** contains reproducible material that makes a compelling case for *why* we should raise

our voices, immediately, on behalf of children.

Chapter 2: What Will We Proclaim? suggests *what* goals, policies, and programs would make the greatest and most critical differences for children. Included in this chapter are a call to action from Marian Wright Edelman and ways CDF is working, in partnership with individuals and groups, to improve the status of children.

Chapter 3: How Can We Make Our Voices Heard? details *how* you can make your voice heard and effective. You will find basic, step-by-step information to help you become a citizen advocate for children through communicating with political candidates, elected officials, and governmental staff.

If you are interested in developing your skills as a public policy advocate for children beyond the level covered in the book, refer to **Section V: Resources to Help You Help Children**. In particular, Chapter 3 provides information about the denominational public policy offices located in Washington, D.C., and some of the national organizations that can provide you with information and put you in touch with others in the community who share your concerns. Chapter 4 lists a variety of publications and videos that may be helpful as you deepen your involvement.

WHY SHOULD WE RAISE OUR VOICES FOR CHILDREN?

Speaking up for our own child or the child of a family we know and love is something we do, often without a second thought. But what about raising our voices for all children — many of whom we don't know and never will see — in the halls of local, state, and federal governments? Why are we called to be public policy advocates for children?

The articles and fact sheets here present information that conveys the urgency of advocating for public policy changes on behalf of our nation's children. Use this material to educate yourself, and duplicate these materials to share with others — as worship bulletin inserts, articles in your church newsletter, or handouts for educational programs and events, for example. The facts about the state of children in America may surprise, and even shock, many. Use this new knowledge to motivate yourself and others into action to change public policies and improve the well-being of our nation's children.

QUESTIONS AND ANSWERS ABOUT AMERICA'S CHILDREN

1. How many American children live in poverty?
2. How many children are homeless in America right now?
3. Are the majority of poor children white or black?
4. Which of these countries has the highest infant mortality rate: Spain, Austria, East Germany, Hong Kong, or the United States?
5. How many children in the United States die every day from the effects of poverty?
6. How many teenagers get pregnant every day?
7. How does America assure that all our children are immunized against childhood diseases?
8. What is the average welfare payment for a destitute family with children?

Answers

1. More than 12 million. **2.** Approximately 100,000. **3.** White. **4.** The United States. **5.** 27. **6.** 2,795. **7.** It doesn't. In 1985, for example, fewer than 80 percent of America's two-year-olds were fully immunized against polio. The rate was lower than in 1980. In 1985 the Reagan Administration stopped collecting data on immunizations. **8.** $4.16 per person per day.

Produced by the Children's Defense Fund, 1991.

U.S. CHILDREN IN THE WORLD

The majority of Americans cling to the notion that children growing up in America are the luckiest and most blessed children in the world. They simply refuse to believe that our wealthy nation is not competitive with other industrialized nations in caring for its children and preparing for its future. The truth is that the United States ranks among the highest nations in the world in per capita gross national product, but does not rank even in the top 10 in any of these measures that are crucial to children's health and well-being.

- American one-year-olds have lower immunization rates against polio than one-year-olds in 14 other countries. Polio immunization rates for nonwhite babies in the United States rank behind the overall rates of 48 countries, including Botswana, Sri Lanka, Albania, Colombia, and Jamaica.
- America's 1987 overall infant mortality rate lagged behind 18 other nations. Our nonwhite infant mortality rate ranked thirtieth compared with other countries' overall rates. A black child born in inner-city Boston has less chance of surviving the first year than a child born in Panama, North or South Korea, or Uruguay.
- In a study of eight industrialized nations (the United States, Switzerland, Sweden, Norway, West Germany, Canada, England, and Australia), America had the highest child poverty rate. Children are the poorest Americans.
- America has the highest teen birth rates among six industrialized nations studied (including France, England and Wales, Canada, the Netherlands, and Sweden).
- America and South Africa are the only industrialized nations that fail to provide universal health coverage, child care, and parental leave for their children and parents.
- America invests a smaller portion of its gross national product (GNP) in child health than 18 other industrialized countries. It invests a smaller proportion of its gross domestic product in education than 13 other industrialized countries.

Produced by the Children's Defense Fund, 1991.

CHILDREN'S DEFENSE FUND

(Cut out and use copies to insert into your church bulletin)

ONE DAY IN THE LIVES OF AMERICA'S CHILDREN

17,051	women get pregnant.
2,795	of them are teenagers.
1,106	teenagers have abortions.
372	teenagers miscarry.
1,295	teenagers give birth
689	babies are born to women who have had inadequate prenatal care.
719	babies are born at low birthweight (less than 5 pounds, 8 ounces).
129	babies are born at very low birthweight (less than 3 pounds, 8 ounces).
67	babies die before one month of life.
105	babies die before their first birthday.
27	children die from poverty.
3	children die from child abuse.
10	children die from guns.
30	children are wounded by guns.
6	teenagers commit suicide.
135,000	children bring guns to school.
7,742	teens become sexually active.
623	teenagers get syphilis or gonorrhea.
211	children are arrested for drug offenses.
437	children are arrested for drinking or drunken driving.
1,512	teenagers drop out of school.
1,849	children are abused or neglected.
3,288	children run away from home.
1,629	children are in adult jails.
2,556	children are born to unmarried women.
2,989	see their parents divorced.
34,285	people lose jobs.
100,000	children are homeless.

Produced by the Children's Defense Fund, 1991.

CHILDREN'S DEFENSE FUND

(Cut out and use copies to insert into your church bulletin)

THE REALITY OF CHILD POVERTY IN AMERICA

Shamal died in New York City. He was eight months old. Cause of death was poverty complicated by low birthweight, poor nutrition, homelessness, and viral infection. During his short life he never slept in an apartment or house; his family was always homeless — he had been in shelters, hospitals, hotels, and the welfare office. He and his mother sometimes rode the subway late at night. Robert Hayes of New York's Coalition for the Homeless said Shamal died because the infant didn't have the strength to resist the "system's abuse."

Baby C was born prematurely with lung disease. His parents lived in a car. His mother received no prenatal care and inadequate nutrition. The family lived on handouts from neighbors and hospital staff. Baby C died at seven months of age in a Michigan hospital. Five days later his mother gave birth prematurely in the car to another baby, who was delivered stillborn. The state paid for a double funeral.

Sally F. and her husband have been separated from their three children for more than three months because they cannot find a place to live. After they lost their apartment because they could not afford the rent increase, the family lived in their car until the weather turned cold. Then, in desperation, the father secretly sheltered his children during the night at the warehouse where he works — stopping when he feared that he would lose his job if discovered. Without a place to live, the parents finally put their children in the temporary care of the state welfare division, which placed them in separate foster homes. The children, still apart, are having increasing problems in school, and their parents have been unable to find an affordable apartment that will accept them and their children. The end of a family life, due to poverty.

Produced by the Children's Defense Fund, 1991.

DEAR LORD BE GOOD TO ME THE SEA IS SO WIDE AND MY BOAT IS SO SMALL

CHILDREN'S DEFENSE FUND

(Cut out and use copies to insert into your church bulletin)

CHILDREN AND THE BUDGET

The budget deficit is the most frequently heard political excuse for neglecting children. Our response is five-fold:

1. Children did not cause the deficit and hurting them more will not cure it.

2. Children and their families have sacrificed proportionately more than any other group — as much as $10 billion per year in the early 1980s in a deficit reduction war in which neither the Pentagon, the rich, nor corporate America were enlisted.

3. Investing in children now saves money later — to fail to prevent sickness, malnutrition, and early childhood deprivation is to perpetuate the very dependency cycle and high remediation costs so many currently decry.

4. Investing in children is feasible and increases our chances of success before problems get serious; we know how to do it and how to achieve positive results for relatively modest investments.

5. Children are dying unnecessarily right now from poverty — one every 53 minutes in America, one every two seconds in the world. How can we dare not to save them if we believe God exists?

Produced by the Children's Defense Fund, 1991.

CHILDREN'S DEFENSE FUND

(Cut out and use copies to insert into your church bulletin)

CHAPTER 2

WHAT WILL WE PROCLAIM?

The problems that too many of our nation's children face are very real — but they can be changed. The Children's Defense Fund is dedicated to working in partnership with individuals, groups, and congregations toward remedies and solutions. The Bible is replete with the images and power of small things that achieve great ends when they are grounded in faith: a mustard seed, a jawbone, a stick, a slingshot, a widow's mite. Each and every one of us can make a difference in the lives of children, if we care enough to empower our compassion with skills, targeted action, and persistence.

In this chapter you will find a call to action from Marian Wright Edelman, the president and founder of the Children's Defense Fund, offering both encouragement and challenge. Next are strategies to improve conditions for America's children — which can only be achieved through the collaboration and mutual dedication of committed advocates for children in churches, schools, businesses, seminaries, and homes across the country. As you begin to advocate for children, consider your particular gifts and talents. How can you use them to work with others to make life better for children in your community and across the nation?

HOW CAN WE
OUR VOICES H

INTRODUCTION

Exodus 5 is the Bible's first record of an advocacy visit. Moses and Aaron go to Pharaoh and ask him to let the Hebrew people take three days for a religious celebration. Pharaoh not only says "No," he orders the overseers "not to supply the people with the straw used in making bricks as they had done hitherto." They still must produce the same quota of bricks but also must spend time gathering the needed straw.

Understandably, the people, flogged, punished, and even more overworked, turn on Moses and Aaron. Moses and Aaron had failed as advocates. When they complain to God, God tells them, "Go [back] and tell Pharaoh king of Egypt to set the Israelites free to leave his country." God gave them the commission to bring the Israelites out of Egypt.

Like Moses and Aaron, when we first venture into advocacy, we may feel inadequate. Like Moses and Aaron, God calls us to go to the powerful and ask for justice though "political realities" would make our request seem outrageously naive. Like Moses and Aaron, though our advocacy is critically important, the outcome does not rest on our efforts alone.

Adapted from Concern Into Action: An Advocacy Guide for People of Faith, *INTERFAITH IMPACT, 1990, Preface*

As citizens of the United States, our task as advocates is much less daunting and, in fact, is protected by the Constitution. In a democracy, we are encouraged to make our concerns known to our elected officials and to candidates for office.

This chapter provides the basic information you need to communicate with your members of Congress on issues affecting children and to make children a priority during the election process.

As Christians, we can use our gift of citizenship in ministry by advocating for those in our society with no power of

their own —
come of our
rest on our e

COMMUN
YOUR ME

Many peopl
process." Ch
all, they are
their needs i
they rush to

Sadly, i
on laws, pro
dren the eas
vote, speak
tions. As a r
not have the

You are
political lif
ally vote for

It's thei
time to writ
tion to their
their local a

Writing
call may see
or tasks, cor
feels more n
need is a litt
this alone. T
to encourag
pose of the
nomination
mobilize co
issues Cong
contact from
organizatio
group. Refe
You Help (

A CALL TO ACTION FROM MARIAN WRIGHT EDELMAN: ALL PEOPLE OF FAITH MUST RAISE THEIR VOICES NOW!

One day, youngsters will learn words they will not understand.
Children from India will ask:
What is hunger?
Children from Alabama will ask:
What is racial segregation?
Children from Hiroshima will ask:
What is the atomic bomb?
Children at school will ask:
What is war?
You will answer them.
You will tell them:
Those words are not used any more
like stage coaches, galleys or slavery
Words no longer meaningful.
That is why they have been removed from dictionaries.
Dr. Martin Luther King, Jr.

We at the Children's Defense Fund seek, with your help, to create a new American paradigm in the 1990s that makes it un-American for any child to grow up poor, unsafe, without basic health care, nutrition, housing, a strong early childhood foundation, and the education they need to earn their share of the American dream.

I believe our nation is at a crossroads of great national opportunity and danger that CDF, in partnership with you in the religious community, must seize now to protect American children, American ideals, and the American future. We can succeed, but only if we mount a massive movement for children strong enough to convince a critical mass of the American public and policy makers to share our belief that the growth of child poverty, drug abuse, violence, and family and neighborhood disintegration in the 1980s pose more of a threat to American prosperity, security, competitiveness, and moral leadership in the new decade than any other enemy outside or inside our borders; and only if we can translate this awareness of child and family crises into real and sustained solutions, rather than symbolic, cosmetic, short-term, politically attractive responses that leave the underlying causes of child poverty and misery substantially unaddressed.

Thanks to the work of child advocates and caring educators and citizens like you, significant progress for children has been made over the past two decades:

- Hundreds of thousands of disabled children now get

a free and appropriate public education, most in mainstream classes;
- Five hundred thousand more mothers now get the prenatal care they need to improve the chances of healthy births;
- One million more low-income children are eligible for basic health care, including preventive check-ups;
- Tens of thousands of neglected, abused, and foster children have the right to decent care while placed outside their parents' home and to services to reunify the family if possible;
- The effective Head Start program has been defended against indiscriminate budget cuts and efforts to weaken its quality;
- Single parents have a greater capacity to secure child support payments from the parent who is not in the home; and
- Families with children are among the protected groups against whom it is prohibited to discriminate in the sale or rental of housing.

And thanks to people like you all over America, children and the nation have gotten off on the right foot in the 1990s with more than $30 billion in new federal investment voted in the 101st Congress to establish a new safe, affordable child care system, toward ensuring a Head Start for every eligible child by 1994, and to provide health care for all poor mothers and children up to age 19.

But these significant gains, which are wonderful but long overdue, are not enough. Our overarching goal must be to eliminate child poverty in this decade.

If we all work together in the 1990s we can begin to rediscover the best of America within ourselves. I would like our children to read in the history books that in the 1990s America came to its senses. Child poverty was wiped out. America stopped clinging to its racial past and recognized that its future was as intertwined with the fate of its poor and nonwhite children as with its privileged and white ones. And, through positive leadership, vision, hard work, and systematic investment in proven strategies, gaps separating minority and poor children from other young Americans were eliminated. As a result, America faced the twenty-first century world with its ideals intact — showing the world through example that all God's children are precious.

We feel confident that we know *what* to do to alleviate child poverty and suffering. The challenge now is *how* to create the political will and sense of urgency to get it done. And that's why your moral witness and hard work are so important.

Marian Wright Edelman

Six Next Steps for Children

The Children's Defense Fund, collaborating with concerned individuals, groups, organizations, and congregations, seeks to ensure that all of our nation's children are given the opportunity to develop to their God-given potential. The following strategies are designed to create a new climate for change and the adoption of critical child investment goals. Working together, we can successfully:

- **Implement massive public education campaigns** through television, Public Service Announcements, billboards, radio, posters, and publications, beginning in 1991, building through the 1992 election year, and continuing until we reach a critical mass of public consciousness and mobilization. Our campaigns are designed to raise consciousness among Americans about how poorly America competes with other in-dustrialized nations in caring for its children, and the threat this poses to every American and the nation's future. As with smoking and the environment, this effort must build cumulatively.

- **Personalize child suffering through a new visitation program** to neonatal intensive care nurseries, home-less shelters, drug-ridden schools and neighbor-hoods, as well as to positive, cost-effective alterna-tives, after careful background briefings. We hope to encourage and train at least 100 communities to adopt the program over the next few years. Its purpose is to create personal awareness and a sense of urgency

PHOTO BY SUSIE FITZHUGH

RESOURCES TO HELP YOU HELP CHILDREN

INTRODUCTION

One of the wonderful things you will discover as you take steps to serve children is the quality and number of individuals, organizations, and resource materials that are available to help you and your congregation. Whether you look within your own congregation, in the community, or to state and national child advocacy organizations, you can find expertise, support, and current resources. Best of all, once you've made some connections, you'll find yourself part of a dynamic and growing network of child advocates and those who care for the well-being of our nation's children.

The purpose of this section is to share some of these resources with you. Keep them in mind as you and your congregation strengthen your ministries to and with children.

Chapter 1: Congregational Model Programs describes many programs housed in congregations or church-supported organizations that successfully meet the needs of children. You will find various models to give you an idea of how congregations that differ in location, size, and amount of resources can make a concrete difference in the lives of children. In most instances a contact person and address are listed, in case you would like more information. We hope this chapter will stimulate your thinking on ways your particular congregation can best utilize its resources to benefit children.

Chapter 2: National Denominational Efforts for Children highlights some advocacy efforts by denominations that are members of the National Council of Churches and also includes the Unitarian Universalist Service Committee. In the past four years, the national denominations have devoted greater attention and resources to children's issues. This intensified focus on children has led to the formation of comprehensive and coordinated child advocacy campaigns and programs.

Chapter 3: Denominational Public Policy Offices and National Organizations lists the denominational public policy offices and some national organizations that focus on children, public policy, poverty, or community organizing.

Your religious denomination may have an office based in Washington, D.C., the staff of which can help you advocate to Congress. Such offices provide denominational members with a variety of programs and resources including legislative alerts, speakers, trainers, telephone consultations on issues, and assistance in setting up congressional visits.

In addition, quite a few national organizations provide information, resources, and technical assistance on programs and policies related to issues affecting children. **Chapter 4: Resources** includes a selection of resources listed by topic. It is not meant to be comprehensive in scope or inclusive of all issues related to children. You will find a few entries under such categories as child advocacy, children and the church, maternal and child health, child care, education, youth self-sufficiency, homelessness and housing, child welfare, and public policy.

ॐ

CONGREGATIONAL MODEL PROGRAMS

CHILD CARE

Congregations Concerned for Children
(A Metropolitan Ecumenical Program)

After holding a series of community hearings on public education, child care, children's health, and child abuse and neglect, the Greater Minneapolis Council of Churches created Congregations Concerned For Children (CCC) in July 1988, with a three-year grant from the McKnight Foundation. A few months later, a twin program began at the St. Paul Area Council of Churches.

The major goals of the CCC program are to create a network of child advocates in religious congregations, to develop partnerships between congregations and child care centers that serve mainly low-income children, and to provide technical consultation to develop new child care centers to serve low-income children in churches.

Child advocacy network

In the first two years of the program, approximately 550 people in congregations have agreed to become child advocates. Almost all of these advocates were recruited in person through adult education programs provided by CCC's speakers bureau. Advocates attend CCC conferences and workshops held throughout the year.

CCC reaches and links these new child advocates through the child advocacy letter (a monthly personal contact) and *The Link* (a bimonthly newsletter).

Partnership

Child care centers that serve mostly children from low-income families face constant financial challenges. They often need new equipment, supplies, and toys. They also need strong board members and people with legal and business expertise. Sometimes the directors of these centers simply need moral support. CCC helps congregations provide these supports through developing partnerships between churches and child care centers.

These church/child care partnerships frequently give volunteers a first, personal experience of the struggles of low-income families served by the child care centers. Often this leads to political advocacy on behalf of children. Through their firsthand experiences at a local child care center, volunteers often learn that without the support of both public and private sectors, the current child care crisis will not be resolved in this century.

Child care consultations

CCC also is working on increasing the supply of child care by providing free consultation services to churches that want to develop new child care centers. CCC staff has created materials that help churches develop child care centers, from the feasibility study stage to the opening of the center. This service, offered free of charge to congregations, is paid for with money provided by the Greater Minneapolis Day Care Association and local architects.

For more information, contact Congregations Concerned for Children, Greater Minneapolis Council of Churches, 122 West Franklin Avenue, Room 218, Minneapolis, MN 55404, (612) 870-3660.

Central Baptist Church's 20
Years of Care for Children

Twenty years ago, Central Baptist Church (Lexington, Kentucky) member Anita Privitt, a mother with young children and later one of the first chairs of the child care committee, was going back to school. She asked the church about beginning a day care program.

"We didn't know the amount of work involved or the regulations we would face to begin a program," she recalled. "It was work and it did create controversy within the church. Some thought the walls would get dirty, and it's true they have been painted many, many times. But we saw it as a mission and a service to meet the need of our members."

Director Betty Morrison says, "We have no advertising, yet we have a waiting list of around 100. We are licensed for 85 in day care and 25 in kindergarten, but because of the space, we serve only about 96 children. Although parents don't have to be Central members to work in the program or for their children to attend, we minister to many of our own.

"We also have a ministry with Central Baptist Hospital and the University of Kentucky Medical Center. We help when a parent is slated for surgery or for a long hospitalization by caring for the patient's children. Sometimes we have to cover the cost of the child care as a part of our commitment to ministry."

Judy Browning, a kindergarten teacher, adds, "Churches have a responsibility to nurture children. A child care center is the greatest way to do that. It provides peace of mind to parents and security to children that they need. Many don't have a secure home life, and for them, this is it."

For more information, contact Central Baptist Church, 1644 Nicholasville Road, Lexington, KY 40503, (606) 278-5913.

EDUCATION

United Methodist Women Local Units' Adopt-A-School Program

Every Monday, from 8 to 9 a.m., Chris Keels has breakfast with some of the children in the federally funded breakfast program at Baltimore's Elmer A. Henderson Elementary School. While they eat, the children chat with Keels about school and what is happening at home. Keels, in turn, tells the children about events in her own life.

Keels is a "Monday morning mentor" from the nearby Christ United Methodist church, which has "adopted" the Henderson School. Church volunteers planned to tutor children but learned that the school really needed volunteers to work with the children's behavior and to expose them to new experiences.

"By talking about our own lives, we try to show them that everyone has difficulties to overcome in life," says Keels. "We tell them that we work hard at our jobs and we expect them to work hard at their job — which is school. We continually say, `We're counting on you to do your best.'"

The Monday morning mentor program is one of several activities started at the inner-city school as part of a six-year Campaign for Children co-sponsored by the United Methodist Women and the Children's Defense Fund.

The volunteers provide cultural excursions once a month to reward students for good behavior in the classroom. The women also initiated a creative dance program that has attracted both boys and girls, a Reading Partners project to help children with reading difficulties, and a neighborhood clean-up project for the whole community on Saturdays.

Principal Anne E. Larkins says the children are responding to the church women's nurturing presence in the school. When a child becomes disruptive in class, a teacher may call the child's volunteer reading partner or a Monday morning mentor and ask her to come to school. "Sometimes," says Keels, "the mentor just sits beside the child in the classroom to help him or her concentrate on school work. Then after school the two of them work on the particular problem."

That approach reduces the number of expulsions and keeps the children from falling behind academically, says Keels. The volunteer also takes the time to feel out the underlying causes of the disruptive behavior. The interaction allows the church to identify families that need assistance from the church or other community organizations.

For more information, contact Christine Keels, United Methodist Women, 12013 Fort Washington Road, Fort Washington, MD 27044, (301) 333-3835.

Operation Getting It Together

This Sebastopol, California, tutoring program teams at-risk students referred by the public schools with older youth outreach workers.

The tutors are paid a modest service allowance that covers the cost of transportation, recreation for the child being tutored, refreshments, and other minor items. Outreach workers who remain in the program for a full year are eligible for Community Service Scholarships of $300 per worker, and the college students who serve in this capacity also can receive college credits for their work.

Often the older youths or administrators of the program are called upon to intervene with and advocate for the child in his or her relationship with the school, and sometimes with the courts, and to assist the child's family in this task. One measure of the success of it is the high number of students who entered the program as children in need of help and are now serving as youth outreach workers.

For more information, contact The Rev. Don Schilling, Operation Getting It Together, 500 North Main Street, Sebastopol, CA 85472, (707) 823-6967.

Vulnerable Children and Families

Adopt a Social Worker Ministry

Connecticut's Adopt a Social Worker ministry provides a structured link between a local religious congregation and the abused and neglected children in the community. The local congregation covenants with a social worker who serves these children and their families. The unmet needs of the children and families (such as food, diapers, or bedding) are identified by the adopted social worker, who describes them to the congregation through a liaison member of the church.

Hundreds of children are helped each month through the ministry, which supports the work of social workers across the state. The ministry gives churches an opportunity to be involved in a valuable and heart-warming outreach mission. It stands as a tangible, growing voice saying that God's people care about poor, abused, and neglected children in their area.

Congregation members respond to the needs of these children through the wealth of caring and goods found among individual members. Good quality used items are shared with those in need. Volunteers from the congregation can contribute some of their time to bake, sew, make simple home repairs, or deliver large items. Some congregations also have been able to provide financial assistance through this ministry to help families needing security deposits, health care, emergency food, or a mover to relocate furniture. Each congregation provides what it is able to and at any time may determine that it cannot meet an identified need.

For more information contact Covenant To Care, Inc., 26 Wintonbury Avenue, Bloomfield, CT 06002, (203) 243-1806.

Homelessness and Housing

Martha's Table

Martha's Table, a Washington, D.C. program serving poor and homeless children and their families, demonstrates the effectiveness of partnerships between child-serving programs and the religious community. Martha's Table is made possible by the 26,000 volunteer hours donated in 1989 by nearly 9,000 volunteers representing a variety of ages and walks of life. It began 10 years ago as a soup kitchen for the homeless and since has expanded to include a variety of programs for poor and homeless children.

The Children's Program offers a variety of programs and activities for children ages five to 14. Children at Martha's Table come from poor homes in the surrounding neighborhood as well as from area shelters for homeless families. More than 18,500 meals and snacks were served to the children in 1989. For many children, the meal they eat at Martha's Table may be the only food they get all day. The need for the program is poignantly evident in the actions of children who have just joined the program — staff often find sandwiches hidden behind books, under cushions on the couch, or at the bottom of toy boxes. New children are afraid there will be no more food when they come back the next day, so they hide a store.

The After-School Drop-in Center run by Martha's Table provides recreational activities for children every weekday from 4 to 6 p.m. Between 30 and 50 children, of whom 70 percent are homeless, are served by the program each day.

The Tutoring Project was serving more than 30 students, each with a personal tutor, less than a year after its initiation in September 1989. Each student and volunteer team meets twice weekly.

The Mother-Toddler Program provides parenting education and literacy sessions, and helps mothers prepare toddlers for school, while the toddlers participate in enrichment activities.

The Summer Program offers recreational and educational activities and nutritious meals daily throughout the summer. In 1989, 676 children came at least once to the program. Seventy-five children participated in a two-week Summer Camp as well.

McKenna's Wagon is the mobile soup kitchen operated by Martha's Table. The wagon distributes 2,100 sandwiches, 50 gallons of soup, beverages, and desserts every day of the year. In the past few years the number of families and children seeking food from the wagon has increased drastically.

Congregations and people of faith supply food, contribute financial support, and provide volunteers as partners with Martha's Table.

For more information contact Pam Selden, Director of Children's Program, Martha's Table, 2124 14th Street, N.W., Washington, DC 20009, (202) 328-6608.

Healthy Baby Weekend

The 1990 Healthy Baby Weekend in Indianapolis is a superb example both of churches advocating on an issue affecting children and of a partnership between religious bodies and a community social action group.

Indianapolis-area church leaders and laity, eager to become involved in social action to reduce their city's continually high infant mortality rate, drafted a Covenant on Infant Mortality. They then forged a partnership with the Indianapolis Campaign for Healthy Babies, which had been eager for the involvement and support of the religious community. Other Indianapolis-area leaders of the Christian, Jewish, and Muslim communities were invited to contribute worship resources for use city-wide in celebrating Healthy Baby Weekend.

The social action and liturgical result was a packet of materials sent to more than 700 area clergy to help their congregations celebrate Healthy Baby Weekend on the third weekend in September. The packet contained:

- A covenant proclaiming Healthy Baby Weekend;
- Sermon and homily notes drawn up on a discussion of the gospel text which the consensus lectionary had designated for the Sunday of Healthy Baby Weekend;
- Sermon and homily suggestions drawing upon other texts, for clergy who do not normally use the lectionary;
- Prayers and litanies;
- A camera-ready list of suggestions for action, for insertion in church bulletins or newsletters; and
- A form to evaluate the usefulness of these worship resources, and to volunteer to contribute worship resources for subsequent Healthy Baby Weekends.

COVENANT ON INFANT MORTALITY

We, the undersigned — as religious communities, as religious leaders, or as individual members of churches, synagogues, mosques, or temples in the Indianapolis area — pledge to commit ourselves, as part of the Covenant on Infant Mortality, to the following:

- To promote Healthy Baby Weekend activities — either coordinated city-wide activities or activities appropriate to our own communities — during the third weekend in September over the next three years (1990-1992);
- To assist the Indianapolis Campaign for Healthy Babies in whatever way possible in reducing the infant mortality rate;
- To work at the local level to reduce the infant mortality rate;
- To monitor annual progress on reducing the overall infant mortality rate as well as the infant mortality rate in the minority communities of Indianapolis; and
- To voice our concerns, as necessary, to civil and civic leaders on matters relating to infant mortality.

We undertake this three-year covenant in atonement for the three previous years in which Indianapolis had one of the highest overall infant mortality rates — and the highest infant mortality rate for African Americans — of any major city in the United States, and in an effort to assist The Indianapolis Campaign for Healthy Babies with the activities it will promote over the next three years.

INDIANAPOLIS' SUGGESTIONS FOR CITIZEN ACTION

1. Donate cribs, car seats, playpens, and other nursery equipment.
2. Volunteer to drive for The Healthy Baby Support Group. You will help mothers to secure adequate prenatal and postnatal care. Call: 638-5677, Monday through Friday mornings, 9 a.m. to noon, to learn more and to volunteer.
3. Write to your city/county councillor, urging him or her to endorse budget appropriations that support The Indianapolis Campaign for Healthy Babies. Call: 236-3600 for the name and address of your councillor.
4. Contact the executive committee of your neighborhood association, encouraging the association to host a WIC (nutrition program for children and pregnant women) clinic or Mom Mobile. No neighborhood should ignore the Indianapolis infant mortality program.
5. For additional information about individual and community needs relating to The Indianapolis Campaign for Healthy Babies, call: (317) 263-4500, or write to: The Indianapolis Campaign for Healthy Babies, 120 West Market Street, Suite 1300, Indianapolis, IN 46204.

With the responses from this last form, the worship coordinators will be able to incorporate suggestions and resources so that subsequent Healthy Baby Weekends may be even more widely celebrated and even more congregations may become informed and involved in increasing the rate of healthy babies born in their city.

For additional information, contact Dr. Ray Marquette, Associate Executive Presbyter, Presbytery of Whitewater Valley, 4900 East 38th Street, Indianapolis, IN 46218, (317) 542-0137, or Mr. Phil McBrien, Director of Religious Education, St. Thomas Aquinas Roman Catholic Church, 4625 North Kenwood Avenue, Indianapolis, IN 46208, (317) 253-1461.

Caring Program for Children

In 1984 two ministers from Pittsburgh, Pennsylvania recognized the growing number of children without health care and decided to do something about it. They approached Blue Cross of Western Pennsylvania and its president to see if something could be done for children whose health care needs were being postponed or neglected when working parents lost their jobs and could not find other work that provided health care benefits.

As a result, Blue Cross of Western Pennsylvania researched this issue, estimating that approximately 40,000 children from low-income families in western Pennsylvania lacked health care coverage.

In response to this need, Blue Cross of Western Pennsylvania together with Blue Shield created the Caring Program for Children. The programs benefits are designed to meet the basic health care needs of children, including preventive care, visits to the doctor when the child is sick, and emergency care. The program is free to the children and their parents. Children are eligible from birth to age 19 if their family income is below the poverty line but above Medicaid guidelines. The cost per year is shared equally by Blue Cross/Blue Shield and a sponsor, such as a congregation, individual, or group. The cost to sponsor a child is less than $200 per year.

"Through the Caring Program for Children and our church, which sponsored Justin, he didn't just get medical care, he got great medical care....Justin had a dozen ear infections a year. With each infection his hearing was always in jeopardy. With the Caring Program, we could take him to our pediatrician. We didn't have to go from clinic to clinic, hospital to hospital, or doctor to doctor.

"Justin was taken to the pediatrician, who knows his problems and his history. His care was consistent. There was a point when we had to rush him to the hospital. Our pediatrician was there. He told us had we waited, Justin could have lost 90 percent of his hearing. That didn't happen, because we had the Caring Program for Children and the consistency of care. It was a godsend and a lifesaver."

Justin's mother

Through a grant from the U.S. Department of Health and Human Services (Maternal and Child Health Division), the Caring Program for Children is being replicated throughout the nation. By mid-1989 the Caring Program was operational in 10 states.

To find out if the Blue Cross/Blue Shield in your area participates in the Caring Program for Children, contact Charles P. LaVallee, Director, Caring Program for Children, 500 Wood Street, Suite 600, Pittsburgh, PA 15222, (412) 687-5437.

YOUTH SELF-SUFFICIENCY

Boys and Babies Program

When Sharon Winkler's son started expressing interest in human sexuality and development, around the age of 12, she realized that she was being presented with a special challenge. She began thinking about what her South Florida community could do to encourage responsible attitudes toward sexuality and parenthood among the city's teenagers. When she discovered that her community did little to educate boys about sexuality, Sharon decided to begin a sexuality education program for preadolescent boys.

Ms. Winkler worked with the Presbyterian Church of the Palms in Sarasota to develop a 12-week course, Boys and Babies, for 12-year-old boys. The course is designed to give the boys experience with babies through an existing child care program. Parents who take their infants to the child care center at the church give permission for their babies to be diapered, fed, and played with by the boys in the class. One parent said, "I think the program is terrific. It's good for the children receiving the care as well as for the staff." But Sharon Winkler also cares about the valuable lessons the experience teaches. "I want the boys to learn to care enough about babies that they won't create one before they're ready," she says.

The program has received positive reactions from the community since it began, seven years ago. The boys themselves are enthusiastic. Dan Hogue didn't want to take the class, but he said, "After a few classes, I really liked it. Mostly we were taking care of babies, but we also saw a couple of films on the stages of life before a baby is born. I think the idea was to teach us this when we're young, so we don't mess up later and get into trouble — like having sex at too early an age."

For more information, contact Ms. Sharon Winkler, 1728 Meadowood Street, Sarasota, FL 34231, (813) 922-7478.

Flowers with Care Youth Services

Flowers with Care Youth Services is run by Father James Harvey, a Roman Catholic priest of the Diocese of Brooklyn. It provides medical and nutritional care, job training, remedial education, counseling, and a sense of self-worth and belonging to troubled young people. It received its unusual name through the first business, a flower shop, that employed the program's first young people.

When young people come to the program, their immediate needs are identified. They receive food, shelter, clothing, and medical care. Pregnant teenagers are directed to the appropriate prenatal services as soon as possible and get help in finding ways to pay for care. Each young person then trains with a corporation or small business, earning the minimum wage. The young person then is given a job with a local business, often a flower shop. At one time, more than 210 florists were working with Father Harvey. Now the types of businesses are more diversified. Though some young people go on to become store managers and owners of flower shops, others choose to attend college or enter other professions.

The program has seen tremendous results in helping young people make a success of their lives. Since 1974 more than 8,000 young people have acquired self-respect, self-confidence, and self-sufficiency through Flowers with Care Youth Services.

For more information, contact The Rev. James Harvey, Flowers with Care Youth Services, 23-40 Astoria Boulevard, Astoria, NY 11102, (718) 726-9790.

NATIONAL DENOMINATIONAL EFFORTS FOR CHILDREN

A GROWING RELIGIOUS MOVEMENT FOR CHILDREN

The increase in child poverty, child abuse and neglect, homelessness, and inadequate health care and education has called the church to a renewal and strengthening of its witness on behalf of children, "the least of these." This commitment stems from the biblical call to exercise compassion in the world.

In coordination with the Children's Defense Fund, national religious denominations and organizations have sought to focus more attention and resources on children's needs and on the networking of their policies and programs related to children. This partnership between the Children's Defense Fund and the religious community builds on each other's strengths so we can multiply our effectiveness in bringing about change for our nation's children.

In this context, major long-term ecumenical and Protestant denominational efforts have been developed to strengthen the community's response to the needs of children and families. While these long-term projects vary in their design and implementation, their goals are the same — to make a positive difference in children's lives. From the United Methodist Women's **Campaign for Children** to the Presbyterian Church (USA) **Five-Year Child Advocacy Program**, these efforts are built on the church's long tradition of ministry to children and the wealth of compassion, experience, and expertise derived from congregations.

This chapter is not meant to be comprehensive in scope. Instead, it focuses on the specific efforts of one particular segment of the religious community — the mainline Protestant denominations and the Unitarian Universalist Service Committee.

Because only a selection of religiously based child advocacy efforts are presented, get in touch with your own denomination — even if it is not mentioned here — to discover what it might have to offer in the area of child advocacy, and to find out how you can become a part of the growing national religious movement for children.

THE NATIONAL COUNCIL OF CHURCHES OF CHRIST

Child and Family Justice Office

The Child and Family Justice Office (formerly called the Child Advocacy Office) of the National Council of Churches of Christ (NCC) has advocated for the rights and well-being of children for more than 12 years. The office grew out of the Child and Family Justice Project, sponsored by the NCC from 1977 to 1980, to identify issues and challenges facing families with young children.

The child advocacy component of the Child and Family Justice Office seeks to:
- Nurture child advocates and educators by offering them leadership training, resources, and technical assistance;
- Lift up justice issues of children and families, especially those who live in poverty; and
- Coordinate and strengthen the ecumenical community's efforts to inform and empower churches to respond to children's needs.

Since its inception, the strength and influence of the NCC's child advocacy work has stemmed from its local base. The office's close relationship with churches and child-serving communities across the country enables it to respond quickly to identify trends and concerns. Through regular and consistent communication with its grassroots base, it gathers data to develop and implement policies and programs.

National Ecumenical Child Care Network

Child care concerns are not of a fleeting nature, but pose enduring issues which reach deep into the nation's life. At the heart of the debate lies the future well-being of America's children and families. The church can enrich and strengthen, as well as gain much from its leadership and participation in, a national dialogue about child care.

National Council of Churches of
Christ,
Policy Statement on Child Day Care

For every child who enters the church on Sunday to attend church school, there are eight children who enter the church on Monday for nurturing, care, and education. Every day of the week more than 2 million children enter churches in America for child care.

This astonishing revelation of the enormous scope of the child care ministry resulted from a 1982 landmark study conducted by the former Child Advocacy Office of the National Council of Churches, with support from the Carnegie and Ford Foundations. The study demonstrated that more than one-third of all out-of-home child care in this country takes place in churches and synagogues. Religious leaders and public policy makers suddenly realized that churches play a leading role in providing high-quality, affordable care for children and in ensuring equitable public child care policies.

The National Council of Churches has worked to enable individual churches to support their child care ministries more effectively. By 1984 the NCC's Ecumenical Child Care Network (ECCN) had identified 14,000 church-housed child care programs. Today, the ECCN is a national, membership-based organization linking more than 1,000 early-childhood and religious educators, congregations, pastors, and child care advocates in action and study to promote high-quality, equitable child care throughout the religious community and the nation.

ECCN members receive a bimonthly newsletter plus regular publications, technical assistance, and leadership training through local and regional affiliates.

Are there children and families in your church or neighborhood who need a quality child care program but have no access to one? If so, the ECCN publishes a step-by-step manual to assist you in planning such a weekday ministry for young children and their families. Does your church now house a nursery school or child care center, Head Start program or after-school care, a day center for children with disabilities, or a parent co-op? The ECCN has self-study and mentor assistance programs to help providers of these and other church-related child care programs.

Child Advocacy Working Group

The Child Advocacy Working Group (CAWG) is the advisory and coordinating body for the child advocacy work of the Child and Family Justice Office. Composed of representatives from many denominations and related child advocacy organizations, CAWG provides an opportunity for its members to learn from each other and to build a coordinated interfaith strategy on children's concerns.

The Ecumenical Child Health Project

As millions of American children suffer the impact of a growing national health crisis, congregations and child care providers have been called on to intervene and try to compensate for inadequate health services. Recognizing the growing and evolving role of churches in assuring health care for our nation's children, the NCC launched in 1989 the first national study of how congregations provide health services for children.

The Ecumenical Child Health Project, an outgrowth of the national survey, is a five-year initiative (1990-1994) designed to improve young children's health by:
- Identifying model health programs operated by or

within churches, and disseminating information about those models to the national church community;

- Increasing church awareness of the scope, danger, and effects of poor child health and what can be done about it; and
- Providing a vehicle within the religious community

to work for public policy changes to ensure good health care for all children.

To join the ECCN network and to order resources, contact the Ecumenical Child Care Network, Child and Family Justice Office, National Council of Churches of Christ, 475 Riverside Drive, Room 572, New York, NY 10115-0050, (212) 870-2664.

The United Methodist Church

Child Advocacy Network

The Child Advocacy Network of the Health and Welfare Ministries Program Department, General Board of Global Ministries, is involved in helping annual conferences establish conference-wide child advocacy networks, and has encouraged each conference to develop those resources which best meet their needs. The networks address critical issues affecting the health and well-being of children, youths, and families. Members of the network become educated about legislation and public policies on federal, state, and local levels. Network members also enable local churches to be in mission on behalf of children and youths. A brochure and booklet on child advocacy will be available sometime in 1991.

For more information, contact the Section on Ministries With Annual Conferences, General Board of Global Ministries, The United Methodist Church, 475 Riverside Drive, Room 350, New York, NY 10115, (212) 870-3910.

Coordinator of Children's Ministries

In response to the need for a comprehensive approach to children's ministries, paragraph 259.1 of the *Book of Discipline* of the United Methodist Church (1988) created a new position at the conference and local church level called the Coordinator of Children's Ministries (Young Children's Education and Ministries, General Board of Discipleship). The coordinator's tasks include helping the church take seriously the needs of children, planning effectively to meet those needs, expanding the ministry of the church with children, increasing the number of options for children within the church, and reaching out into the community to participate with others for the good of children.

For more information, contact the Young Children's Education and Ministries, General Board of Discipleship, The United Methodist Church, P.O. Box 840, Nashville, TN 37202-0840, (615) 340-7170.

United Methodist Women

Campaign For Children

TO: United Methodist Women in Every Local
       Church
FR: Theresa Hoover, [Former] Deputy General
       Secretary
       The Women's Division
       General Board of Global Ministries
DATE: August, 1987
RE: A Continuing Mission

Have you ever wished for an opportunity to do a "hands-on" mission task? Well, now you can stop the search!

The Women's Division, in cooperation with the Children's Defense Fund, has developed a plan, which we think will speak to the desires of local United Meth-

odist Women, for "hands-on" mission experiences. We call it a Campaign for Children....

Who can look in the face of a child — any child — and not remember that that face is a reminder that God the Creator has not despaired of humanity. Whether parent, grandparent, aunt, or simply a responsible adult, each of us is called to give voice to the voiceless in our midst — children!

This invitation to action heralded the beginning of the United Methodist Women's Campaign for Children. The six-year campaign (1988-1993) is designed to help United Methodist Women's (UMW) Local Units make a concrete difference in children's lives. Its goal is to empower new and effective UMW child advocates by developing appropriate education and training resources, innovative projects and programs that work, and a vehicle for communicating with the growing UMW child advocacy network.

Beginning in January 1988, the campaign called on each of the 30,000 UMW Local Units to study the status of children in their community and to take action through community service and political advocacy. The campaign urged UMW Local Units to involve the entire congregation in their activities and to join with other community groups and churches for community-wide public awareness and action.

To prepare Local Units to act for children, in 1988 the Women's Division and the Children's Defense Fund jointly developed an information and action kit which was sent to each Local Unit president. The packet contained a study and action guide, bulletin inserts, and a commitment form. In 1989 the Women's Division produced a training video, "To Love in Deed," to help UMW units move forward on activities and programs in their own communities. Two copies of this inspiring 30-minute video were distributed by the Women's Division to each annual conference president.

In the initial years of the Campaign for Children, the Women's Division collected and studied the Local Units' completed commitment forms to assess the level of activity and additional tools they would need to begin or continue their efforts. An informal communique is sent to each responding Local Unit several times a year, keeping them informed and sharing successful projects and ideas.

In addition to initiating local action, the Campaign for Children organized a grassroots advocacy initiative which generated thousands upon thousands of letters, postcards, and calls to members of Congress, urging them to pass a child care bill to benefit low- to middle-income families. For example, 10,000 postcards to President Bush, urging him to sign the child care bill, were collected at the 1990 Women's Division Assembly in Kansas City, and later presented to the White House.

In the next few years the Campaign for Children will build on existing efforts to continually enhance and increase the work of the Local Units in their communities on behalf of children. This will include working with CDF to produce an updated version of the Campaign for Children booklet and packet materials, to implement grassroots legislative initiatives on timely issues, and to develop the UMW child advocacy network. In 1993, the final year of the official campaign, the United Methodist Women will celebrate six years of accomplishments and lay the groundwork for the future. The Women's Division will organize and promote a UMW national gathering on the Campaign for Children, bringing together UMW Local Units from around the country to share successful projects and local partnerships, evaluate their progress, and map out a follow-up strategy.

For more information, contact Chiquita Smith, Secretary For Community Action, Women's Division, General Board of Global Ministries, The United Methodist Church, 475 Riverside Drive, 15th Floor, New York, NY 10115-0050, (212) 870-3766.

PRESBYTERIAN CHURCH (USA)

Child Advocacy Project

It is imperative that we act now to accelerate the pace and rate of change. For children there can be no further delay in providing optimum conditions for the fulfillment of human potential. The future of the child is now....The church must continue...to support and undergird the efforts which would enable each child to become an inheritor of the kingdom.

Thelma Adair
General Moderator of the
188th General Assembly
Presbyterian Church (USA)

Frustrated and deeply saddened by the status of children in the United States and the world, in 1988 staff members at the General Assembly level of the church developed a proposal to engage "the Presbyterian Church (USA), its governing bodies and its members, in child advocacy to fulfill its baptismal commitments through education, service and networking." The proposal was submitted to the Presbyterian Women's Birthday Offering, which recognized the critical need and responded by fully funding the project for 1990 through 1994.

The Child Advocacy Project (CAP) Committee was established to implement the project and included staff from three ministry units (Education and Congregational Nurture, Social Justice and Peacemaking, and Women's), with a local church member as moderator.

The committee's first task was to find out what was happening in the local churches and what they needed to be more effective advocates for children. To accomplish this, a call for participants to a conference was made to the 16 synods (regional governing bodies). More than 130 people, representing every synod, gathered in Tampa, Florida, for reflection, education, and discussion, and are the core of an emerging child advocacy network.

Informed by the participants' ideas, the CAP committee developed a comprehensive five-year plan, which focuses on service, education, and networking. Forming partnerships with other ecumenical and secular child advocacy groups is a vital part of the work. The Children's Defense Fund, the Child and Family Justice Office of the National Council of Churches, the Ecumenical Child Care Network, and others have worked closely to support and develop the project.

The Child Advocacy Project of the Presbyterian Church (USA) is underway and building momentum. To become a part of the Presbyterian Child Advocacy Network, or for more information, contact the Child Advocacy Project, Presbyterian Church (USA), 100 Witherspoon Street, Room 3066, Louisville, KY 40202-1396, (503) 569-5792.

THE EPISCOPAL CHURCH

The Children's Advocacy Committee

In our Baptismal Covenant we are called to strive for justice among all people, and respect the dignity of every human being. We must not forget the children of our society as we seek to fulfill our Baptismal Covenant as the People of the Resurrection.

The Most Rev. Edmond Browning
Presiding Bishop

The Children's Advocacy Committee (CAC) of the Episcopal Church, working through the Office of Social Welfare at the Episcopal Church Office in New York, was established by the General Convention in 1988. The committee affirms the Episcopal Church's commitment to all children and seeks to involve congregations in addressing the issues of child abuse, child care, child welfare, family support, education, and public policy.

CAC is made up of leaders and professionals whose ministries support and enhance the well-being of children. Members represent such disciplines as mental health, social welfare, disability concerns, education, health, and child welfare.

The mandate of the Children's Advocacy Committee is to:

- Strengthen and expand ministry to children, while building networks among Christian educators, social service agencies, and advocacy groups;
- Educate and train local and regional church staff and members to act on behalf of children;
- Develop an Episcopal children's advocacy network composed of parish, diocesan, and national church leaders; and
- Advocate for children by influencing federal and state legislation related to child care, child health, education, and child welfare.

Since its inception, the Children's Advocacy Committee members have been working to provide Episcopalians with the resources and support necessary to meet children's needs in their communities. It has conducted a survey of all congregations to prepare a directory of child care programs housed in an Episcopal church; published and distributed a brief report, *The Children's Advocate*; and made presentations at the Families 2000 Project, 1990, of the Episcopal Church.

Those interested in becoming involved in the work of the CAC are encouraged to write for more information to the Office of Social Welfare, Episcopal Church Center, 815 Second Avenue, New York, NY 10017, (212) 867-8400 ext. 289.

THE EVANGELICAL LUTHERAN CHURCH IN AMERICA

Our Children At Risk Series: Hope For Our Future Together

To help its more than 11,000 congregations extend their commitment to biblical study, evangelism, and service in the world throughout the 1990s, the Evangelical Lutheran Church in America (ELCA) developed a church-wide emphasis called Mission 90. Our Children At Risk: Hope For Our Future Together is one part of the third phase of Mission 90. This multi-generational resource is designed to assist all ELCA congregations in looking at the themes of peace, justice, and care of creation through the eyes of children at risk in our society and in our world.

Our Children At Risk: Hope For Our Future Together is a 12-session written resource that helps children, youths, and adults relate the themes of peace, justice, and care of creation to the various spheres of their daily life, congregation, and their immediate and global communities. The hope is that all ages will explore together the issues that touch their lives, gain a greater awareness of the situations and problems children face, and work together to advocate for children locally and around the world. A leader guide will be available in the fall of 1991.

For more information, contact the Specialist for Children's Education, Division for Congregational Life, Evangelical Lutheran Church in America, 8765 W. Higgins Road, Chicago, IL 60631, (800) 638-3522 ext. 2556.

THE UNITED CHURCH OF CHRIST

Who Speaks for the Children?

In September 1986 the Office for Church in Society of the United Church of Christ invited representatives of denominations, ecumenical agencies, child advocacy groups, and organizations helping low-income persons to join with them in a national ecumenical effort called Who Speaks for the Children. A National Planning Committee on Children in Poverty was formed to develop and implement an ecumenical effort to support public policies at all levels of government that benefit children and families, especially those in need, and to include the grassroots participation of low-income families.

The Who Speaks for the Children campaign began with regional hearings on child poverty in five cities around the country, to focus local attention on the needs of children, recommend solutions, and mobilize local support. From the fall of 1987 to the winter of 1988, more than 1,000 poor children, mothers, families, and their representatives (such as community organizations, advocacy groups, and social service providers) participated. State legislators, social service provid-ers, city administrators, low-income mothers, and others shared their stories about child and family poverty and recommended ways to address the problem. The local planning team in Iowa produced a 20-minute video of the hearings.

The culminating event for the regional hearings was the National Consultation on Children in Poverty, which was held in Washington, D.C., in February 1988. A focal point was testimony presented to members of the House Select Committee on Children, Youth and Families by a few of the regional hearing coordinators and participants.

Since then representatives from the National Planning Committee and the regional hearings have met annually to organize further national and local activities that continue to shape public policies for children and families. A major goal of the meetings and activities is to forge a partnership with low-income families in the national and local efforts to address child poverty and in state and national decision-making on public policies related to children and families.

For more information about this ongoing effort, contact Becky Gallatin, The United Church of Christ, Office for Church in Society, 110 Maryland Avenue, N.E., Washington, DC 20002, (202) 543-1517.

UNITARIAN UNIVERSALIST SERVICE COMMITTEE

Focus on Children in the 1990s

Upon this gifted age, in its dark hour,
Falls from the sky a meteoric shower
Of facts...they lie unquestioned, uncombined
Wisdom enough to leech us of our ill
is daily spun, but there exists no loom
To weave it into fabric...

Edna St. Vincent Millay

Information about America's children abounds. One in five lives in poverty. One in six has no medical insurance. One in seven may not complete high school. Tens of thousands are homeless, their numbers increasing....The questions that such information raises about our society and our future demand response. Our challenge is to begin a process of inquiry and build a loom of understanding so that together we can, as the poet says, weave the facts into a fabric of wisdom — a fabric for action.

From Promise The Children
UUSC's study guide on the rights and needs of children

The Unitarian Universalist Service Committee (UUSC) is an independent, nonsectarian membership organization that promotes peace, justice, and freedom in the United States and around the world.

Because the UUSC is committed to seeking a better life for children in the United States, it has embarked on a pro-gram focused on the rights and needs of children, especially those in poverty. Over the next decade, the UUSC will build partnerships with Unitarian Universalists and their congregations to advocate for an enlightened government policy toward children. The agency will provide educational and policy resources and work with partner congregations to develop effective citizen education and action programs.

The UUSC monitors selected national legislation affecting children and provides constituents with "action alerts" outlining key bills pending in Congress. The alerts encourage members of congregations throughout the country to write or call their elected representatives, hold public forums or town meetings, or visit their representatives' offices.

The UUSC will assist partner congregations in working on behalf of children in their communities. Congregational projects will be tailored to local needs and to each congregation's readiness to mobilize for action.

It also provides constituents with educational materials including fact sheets, background reports, bibliographies, and issue analyses that examine the problems faced by children at risk. In its first year, the children's program concentrated on child care, Head Start, and the federal Special Supplemental Food Program for Women, Infants, and Children (WIC). In subsequent years the program will tackle issues such as education, homelessness, poverty, and discrimination.

For more information and to receive the UUSC's legislative action alerts, contact the Unitarian Universalist Service Committee, 130 Prospect Street, Cambridge, MA 02139-1813, (617) 868-6600.

DENOMINATIONAL PUBLIC POLICY OFFICES AND NATIONAL ORGANIZATIONS

DENOMINATIONAL PUBLIC POLICY OFFICES

AMERICAN BAPTIST CHURCHES, USA
Office of Governmental Relations
110 Maryland Avenue, N.E., Suite 511
Washington, DC 20002
(202) 544-3400

CHRISTIAN CHURCH (DISCIPLES OF CHRIST)
Department of Church in Society P.O. Box 1986
222 S. Downey Avenue
Indianapolis, IN 46206
(317) 353-1491, ext. 374

CHURCH OF THE BRETHREN
110 Maryland Avenue, N.E., Box 50
Washington, DC 20002
(202) 546-3202

CHURCH WOMEN UNITED
Washington Office:
110 Maryland Avenue, N.E.
Washington, DC 20002
(202) 544-8747

New York Office:
475 Riverside Drive, Room 812
New York, NY 10115-0050
(212) 870-2347

THE EPISCOPAL CHURCH
Washington Office:
110 Maryland Avenue, N.E.
Washington, DC 20002
(202) 547-7300   (800) 228-0515

EPISCOPAL CHURCH PUBLIC POLICY NETWORK
PUBLIC MINISTRIES CLUSTER
The Episcopal Church Center
815 Second Avenue
New York, NY 10017
(212) 867-8400   (800) 334-7626

EVANGELICAL LUTHERAN CHURCH IN AMERICA
Office for Governmental Affairs
122 C Street, N.W., Suite 300
Washington, DC 20001
(202) 783-7507

FRIENDS COMMITTEE ON NATIONAL LEGISLATION (FCNL)
245 2nd Street, N.E.
Washington, DC 20002
(202) 547-6000

JESUIT SOCIAL MINISTRIES, NATIONAL OFFICE
1424 16th Street, N.W., #300
Washington, DC 20036
(202) 462-7008

NATIONAL COUNCIL OF CHURCHES
110 Maryland Avenue, N.E.
Washington, DC 20002
(202) 544-2350

NETWORK: A NATIONAL CATHOLIC SOCIAL JUSTICE LOBBY
806 Rhode Island Avenue, N.E.
Washington, DC 20018
(202) 526-4070

PRESBYTERIAN CHURCH (USA)
110 Maryland Avenue, N.E., Box 52
Washington, DC 20002
(202) 543-1126

UNITARIAN UNIVERSALIST ASSOCIATION OF CONGREGATIONS (UUA)
100 Maryland Avenue, N.E., #106
Washington, DC 20002
 (202) 547-0254

UNITARIAN UNIVERSALIST SERVICE COMMITTEE
2000 P Street, N.W., Suite 515
Washington, DC 20036
(202) 387-4587

OFFICE FOR CHURCH IN SOCIETY
UNITED CHURCH OF CHRIST (UCC)
110 Maryland Avenue, N.E.
Washington, DC 20002
(202) 543-1517

BOARD OF CHURCH & SOCIETY
UNITED METHODIST CHURCH
100 Maryland Avenue, N.E.
Washington, DC 20002
(202) 488-5600

WOMEN'S DIVISION
GENERAL BOARD OF GLOBAL MINISTRIES
UNITED METHODIST CHURCH
100 Maryland Avenue, N.E., Box 56
Washington, DC 20002
(202) 488-5660

National Organizations

AMERICAN ACADEMY OF PEDIATRICS
1331 Pennsylvania Avenue, N.W., Suite 721 North
Washington, DC 20004
(202) 662-7460

BREAD FOR THE WORLD
802 Rhode Island Avenue, N.E.
Washington, DC 20018
(202) 269-0200

CENTER ON BUDGET AND POLICY PRIORITIES
777 North Capitol Street, N.E., Suite 705
Washington, DC 20002
(202) 408-1080

CHILD WELFARE LEAGUE OF AMERICA
440 First Street, N.W., Suite 310
Washington, DC 20001
(202) 638-2952

CHILDREN'S DEFENSE FUND
122 C Street, N.W.
Washington, DC 20001
(202) 628-8787

CHURCHES' CENTER FOR THEOLOGY AND
PUBLIC POLICY
4500 Massachusetts Avenue, N.W.
Washington, DC 20016
(202) 885-9100

COALITION ON HUMAN NEEDS
1000 Wisconsin Avenue, N.W.

Washington, DC 20007
(202) 342-0726

FOOD RESEARCH AND ACTION CENTER (FRAC)
1875 Connecticut Avenue, N.W., Suite 540
Washington, DC 20009
(202) 986-2200

HABITAT FOR HUMANITY INTERNATIONAL
121 Habitat Street
Americus, GA 31709
(912) 924-6935

INTERFAITH IMPACT
100 Maryland Avenue, N.E.
Washington, DC 20002
(202) 544-8636

THE MIDWEST ACADEMY
225 West Ohio Street, Suite 250
Chicago, IL 60610
(312) 645-6010

NATIONAL ASSOCIATION FOR THE EDUCATION
OF YOUNG CHILDREN
1834 Connecticut Avenue, N.W.
Washington, DC 20009-5786
(202) 232-8777

NATIONAL BLACK CHILD DEVELOPMENT
INSTITUTE
1463 Rhode Island Avenue, N.W.
Washington, DC 20005
(202) 387-1281

NATIONAL COALITION FOR THE HOMELESS
1621 Connecticut Avenue, N.W., 4th Floor
Washington, DC 20009
(202) 265-2371

NATIONAL COUNCIL OF LA RAZA
810 First Street, N.E.
Washington, DC 20002-4205
(202) 289-1380

NATIONAL LOW INCOME HOUSING COALITION
1012 14th Street, N.W., #1500
Washington, DC 20005
(202) 662-1530

U.S. COMMITTEE FOR UNICEF
110 Maryland Avenue, N.E., Room 304
Washington, DC 20002
(202) 547-7946

RESOURCES

Addresses and telephone numbers are provided for those resources that may not be available in a library. Contact the publisher directly for more information.

CHILD ADVOCACY

Children's Defense Fund. *An Advocate's Guide to Fund Raising*. Washington, DC: CDF, 1990.

Children's Defense Fund. *An Advocate's Guide to the Media*. Washington, DC: CDF, 1990.

Children's Defense Fund. *An Advocate's Guide to Using Data*. Washington, DC: CDF, 1990.

Fernandez, Happy Craven. *The Child Advocacy Handbook*. New York: The Pilgrim Press, 1980.

Unitarian Universalist Service Committee. *Promise the Children Guidebook*. 1990. Available from: UUSC, 130 Prospect Street, Cambridge, MA 02139-1813, (617) 868-6600.

United Methodist Women. *Campaign for Children Packet*. 1988. Available from: UMW's Campaign for Children, Service Center, 7820 Reading Road, Caller No. 1800, Cincinnati, OH 45222-1800.

United Voices for Children. *Handbook for the Child Advocate*. Available from United Voices for Children, 1580 N. Northwest Highway, Suite 111, Park Ridge, IL 60068.

CHILD CARE

Children's Defense Fund. *Child Care: The Time is Now*. Washington, DC: CDF, 1987.

Children's Defense Fund. *Who Knows How Safe? The Status of State Efforts to Ensure Quality Child Care*. Washington, DC: CDF, 1990.

Freeman, Margery, ed. *Called to Act: Stories of Child Care Advocacy in Our Churches*. 1986. Available from: Child and Family Justice Office, National Council of Churches of Christ, 475 Riverside Drive, New York, NY 10115-0050, (212) 870-2664.

National Council of Churches of Christ. *Helping Churches Mind the Children: A Guide for Church-Housed Child Care Programs*. Rev. ed. 1987. Available from: Child and Family Justice Office, NCC.

National Council of Churches of Christ. *National Council of Churches of Christ Policy Statement on Child Day Care*. 1984. Available from: Child and Family Justice Office, NCC.

Steele, Dorothy M., ed. *Congregations and Child Care: A Self-Study for Churches and Synagogues and Their Early Childhood Programs*. 1990. Available from: Child and Family Justice Office, NCC.

CHILD WELFARE

Edna McConnell Clark Foundation. *Keeping Families Together: Facts on Family Preservation Services*. Information kit. Available from: Edna McConnell Clark Foundation, Communications Department, 250 Park Avenue, New York, NY 10177-0026, (212) 986-7050.

National Crime Prevention Council. *Mission Possible: Churches Supporting Fragile Families*. Washington, DC: 1990. For information, contact: Maria Nagorski, Director, Technical Assistance Center, NCPC, 1700 K Street, N.W., 2nd Floor, Washington, DC 20007, (202) 466-6272.

CHILDREN AND THE CHURCH

Blazer, Doris A., ed. *Faith Development in Early Childhood.* Kansas City, MO: Sheed and Ward, 1989.

Coles, Robert. *The Spiritual Life of Children.* Boston: Houghton Mifflin, 1990.

Glass, Dorlis Brown. *Children, Children: A Ministry Without Boundaries.* Available from: General Board of Discipleship, United Methodist Church, P.O. Box 189, Nashville, TN 37202-0840, (615) 340-7285.

Norton, MaryJane Pierce. *Your Job as a Children's Coordinator.* Available from: General Board of Discipleship, United Methodist Church.

CHILDREN AND POVERTY

Barrett, John M. *It's Hard Not to Worry: Stories for Children About Poverty.* New York: Friendship Press, 1988.

Brazelton, T. Berry. "Why is America Failing Its Children?" *New York Times Magazine,* September 9, 1990.

Coles, Robert. *Children of Crisis.* Boston: Little, Brown & Co.
Vol. 1, *A Study of Courage and Fear,* 1977.
Vol. 2, *Migrants, Sharecroppers, Mountaineers,* 1973.
Vol. 3, *The South Goes North,* 1973.
Vol. 4, *Eskimos, Chicanos, Indians* (not in *Books in Print*)
Vol. 5, *Privileged Ones: The Well-off and the Rich in America,* 1980.

Edelman, Marian Wright. *Families in Peril: An Agenda for Social Change.* Cambridge: Harvard University Press, 1987.

Schorr, Lisbeth. *Within Our Reach: Breaking the Cycle of Disadvantage.* New York: Anchor Press, 1988.

United Church of Christ. *Proceedings of the National Consultation on Children in Poverty.* 1988. Available from: Office for Church in Society, United Church of Christ, 700 Prospect Avenue, Cleveland, OH 44115.

EDUCATION

Children's Defense Fund. *An Advocate's Guide to Improving Education.* Washington, DC: CDF, 1990.

United Church Board for Homeland Ministries. *Models of Service and Replicable Programs in Support of Public Education, 1988-1989.* Available from: Division of the American Missionary Association, UCBHM, 700 Prospect Avenue, Cleveland, OH 44115.

HOMELESSNESS AND HOUSING

Children's Defense Fund. *Your Family's Rights Under the New Fair Housing Law.* Washington, DC: CDF, 1989.

Churches Conference on Shelter and Housing. *Building on Faith: Models of Church-Sponsored Affordable Housing Programs in the Washington, D.C. Area.* 1989. Available from: CCSH, 1711 14th Street, N.W., Washington, DC 20009.

Kozol, Jonathan. *Rachel and Her Children: Homeless Families in America.* New York: Fawcett Columbine, 1988.

McDaniels, James A., ed. *Homelessness and Affordable Housing, A Resource Book for Churches.* 1989. Available from: United Church Board for Homeland Ministries, United Church of Christ, 700 Prospect Avenue, Cleveland, OH 44115.

HOW TO AFFECT NATIONAL PUBLIC POLICY

Children's Defense Fund. *A Children's Defense Budget.* Washington, DC: CDF, annual publication.

Children's Defense Fund. *CDF's Nonpartisan Congressional Voting Record.* Washington, DC: CDF, annual publication.

Clarke, Tina. *Concern Into Action: An Advocacy Guide for People of Faith.* 1990. Available from: INTERFAITH IMPACT, 100 Maryland Avenue, N.E., Washington, DC 20002, (202) 544-8636.

Unitarian Universalist Service Committee. *The Busy Person's Guide to Social Action.* Rev. ed. 1990. Available from: UUSC, 130 Prospect Street, Cambridge, MA 02139-1813, (617) 868-6600.

INTERNATIONAL ISSUES

Castell, Kay. *In the Child's Best Interest, A Primer on the U.N. Convention on the Rights of the Child.* 1988. Available from: Foster Parents Plan International, 804 Quaker Lane, East Greenwich, RI 02818; or: Defense for Children International, 210 Forsyth Street, New York, NY 10002.

Grant, James D. *The State of the World's Children 1991.* New York: United Nations Children's Fund/Oxford University Press, 1990.

MATERNAL AND CHILD HEALTH

Booth, Beverly E., comp. *Striving for Fullness of Life: The Church's Challenge in Health — A Compilation of Health-Related Church Models, A Pilot Study.* 1989. For information, contact: Carter Center of Emory University, 1 Copenhill, Atlanta, GA 30307, (404) 420-5151; or: Wheat Ridge Foundation, 104 South Michigan Avenue, Chicago, IL 60603, (312) 263-1182.

Caring Program for Children. *Health Care for Children in Need.* Pamphlet. Contact: Charles P. LaVallee, Director, P.O. Box Caring, Pittsburgh, PA 15230, (412) 687-5437.

Children's Defense Fund. *The Health of America's Children.* Washington, DC: CDF, annual publication.

VIDEOS

Children's Defense Fund. *When I Dream: Examining the Nation's Teenage Pregnancy Problem.* Washington, DC: CDF, 1988.

Congregations Concerned for Children. *A Better Chance for Children.* Updated 1990. Rental or purchase from: CCC, 122 W. Franklin Avenue, #218, Minneapolis, MN 55404, (612) 870-3660.

Iowa Inter-Church Agency for Peace and Justice. *Who Speaks for the Children?* 1988. Available from: Office for Church in Society, United Church of Christ, 700 Prospect Avenue, Cleveland, OH 44115.

National Council of Churches. *America's Children: Poorest in a Land of Plenty.* 1989. Available from: Ecufilm, P.O. Box 320, Nashville, TN 37202-0320, (800) 251-4091.

National Council of Churches. *A Place for Growing: Child Care in the Church.* 1985. Available for rental from: Child and

Family Justice Office, NCC, 475 Riverside Drive, New York, NY 10115-0050, (212) 870-2664.

Unitarian Universalist Service Committee. *Promise the Children.* 1990. Available from: UUSC, 130 Prospect Street, Cambridge, MA 02139-1813, (617) 868-6600.

United Methodist Women. *To Love in Deed: United Methodist Women's Campaign for Children.* 1989. Available from: Ecufilm.

WORSHIP RESOURCES

Anderson, Yohann, ed. *Songs.* Available from: Songs and Creations, Inc., P.O. Box 7, San Anselmo, CA 94960.

Congregations Concerned for Children. *Recognizing and Celebrating Children.* 1990. Available from: CCC, 122 W. Franklin Avenue, #218, Minneapolis, MN 55404, (612) 870-3660.

Weems, Ann. *Reaching for Rainbows: Resources for Creative Worship.* Philadelphia, PA: Westminster Press, 1980.

YOUTH SELF-SUFFICIENCY AND TEEN PREGNANCY PREVENTION

Children's Defense Fund. *The Adolescent and Young Adult Fact Book.* Washington, DC: CDF, 1991.

Children's Defense Fund. *Adolescent Pregnancy Prevention Clearinghouse.* Washington, DC: CDF, six issues per year. Recent issues include:
- *Improving Health Programs for Low-income Youths* (July 1990)
- *Latino Youths at a Crossroads* (January/March 1990, double issue)
- *Where to Find Data About Adolescents and Youths: A Guide to Sources* (November 1989)
- *Evaluating Your Adolescent Pregnancy Program: How to Get Started* (September 1989)
- *Lack of Health Insurance Makes a Difference* (July 1989)
- *Service Opportunities for Youth* (May 1989)
- *Tackling the Youth Employment Problem* (March 1989)
- *Lessons of Multi-Site Initiatives Serving High-Risk Youths* (January 1989)
- *What About the Boys? Teenage Pregnancy Prevention Strategies* (July 1988)
- *Making the Middle Grades Work* (September 1988)
- *Teens and AIDs: Opportunities for Prevention* (November 1988)

Cellman, Carol D. and Peggy L. Halsey. *Children and Youth in Jeopardy, A Mission Concern for United Methodists.* Rev. ed. 1990. Available from: Service Center, National Program Division, General Board of Global Ministries, The United Methodist Church, 7820 Reading Road, Caller No. 1800, Cincinnati, OH 45222-1800.

Dryfoos, Joy G. *Adolescents at Risk: Prevalence and Prevention.* New York: Oxford University Press, 1990.

National Academy of Sciences. *Risking the Future: Adolescent Sexuality, Pregnancy, and Child Bearing* (two volumes). Washington, DC: National Academy Press, 1986.

Youth Workers Network for Peace and Justice. *Youthpeace.* Quarterly publication. Available from: Institute for Peace and Justice, 4144 Lindell Boulevard, #122, St. Louis, MO 63108.

READERS' SURVEY

Your assistance in evaluating this guide will help us prepare improved materials for congregations. Please complete this questionnaire, detach, and mail in an envelope to CDF, Attn: Kathleen Guy, 122 C Street, N.W., Washington, DC 20001. To show our appreciation for your response, we will send you CDF's 1990 publication, *An Advocate's Guide to Fund Raising.*

Listed below are the five sections in this book. Please indicate how helpful each is to you as you seek ways to lift up and act upon the needs of children in your congregation, community, and around the nation.

	Not Very Helpful	Somewhat Helpful	Very Helpful	Did Not Use	Comments
Section I: The Eyes of Faith					
Section II: Step By Step					
Section III: Study Into Action					
Section IV: Giving Voice to the Voiceless					
Section V: Resources					

1. What was missing for you?

2. What was most useful?

3. What would you change or add?

Your name and (optional) position in the church/group: _____

Address and phone number:_____

_____

_____

Church's name, address, and phone number (if appropriate or different from above):

_____

_____

_____

Denomination (optional): _____

❑ Yes, I would like to become part of a growing network of advocates for children. Let my denomination know of my interest, and keep me informed of model programs and activities for churches, resources, events, and legislative updates.